Advance praise

"We doubled our top-line revenue in the year following our implementation of *The Machine* and are applying these same concepts to an international company we just acquired and seeing the same sort of gains in effectiveness. Justin's book is providing us with an even deeper understanding of the principles that changed our company and continue to drive our sales."

—Aubrey Meador, President of ARCA

"There's no reason for the sales department to be the least predictable and most chaotic part of a company. *The Machine* brings order by removing non-sales work from salespeople and replacing it with centralized scheduling, standardized workflows, specialized resources and formalized management. *The Machine* offers a proven system for growing sales in an organized, consistent way."

—Andrew Warner, Founder of Mixergy

"The pioneering work of Justin Roff-Marsh in the design and execution of effective sales 'machines' is, in my view, world leading. Organizations who ignore it in the connected, globally competitive twenty-first century do so at their peril."

—John Lyons, independent company director
and coauthor of *Marketing without Money*

"In his provocative book, *The Machine*, Justin Roff-Marsh has thoughtfully and forcefully challenged the status quo as it pertains to the design of the sales function. Some readers will be angry, some dismissive, and a select few will be enlightened by this alternative approach. We fall in the latter camp and have found Justin's approach to be a true asset for growing sales in today's complex selling environment!"

—Mike Schleyhahn, President of Swagelok San Diego

"*The Machine* will challenge everything you know about the sales process! It makes a lot of sense, passes all the logical tests, and in the end, might just keep you awake at night. We worked hard to implement a number of these concepts in our organization and I can attest that the ideas are valid and the payoffs are real."

—Jeff Stuart, President of Hydra-Power Systems Inc.

"Justin's approach to addressing the tired structure of traditional sales environments is nothing short of revolutionary. *The Machine* shows management how to drive growth with a tightly synchronized machine, as an alternative to herding individual salespeople. There's no question that this book will be a great investment for any executive that runs a sales team."

—Paul O'Dwyer, author and business growth coach

"Justin's book is a delight. Justin translates the idea that the whole is greater than the sum of its parts to sales, demonstrating that there is a substantially better way to sell compared to simply summing the sales of each salesperson in a team."

—Humberto R. Baptista, CEO of Vectis-Solutions
and lecturer at TOC Schools

"As an operations guy, I'm driven by process, efficiency, and repeatability. The notion that the sales function is an art immune from the rigors of process has never sat well with me. *The Machine* shatters that myth. *The Machine* is a must read for any business leader wanting to achieve predictable results from their sales function."

—Marc Allman, COO of AMS Controls

"Justin Roff-Marsh gets to the root causes of underperforming sales quickly and succinctly. It is clear he knows sales inside and out and has thought deeply about the profession's problems. The book is both global in its implications for sales and practical in its applications for selling."

—Charles Coury, President of 9Wood

"We have worked with Justin and his team for the past seven months and I am continually impressed with the team's professionalism and knowledge. I am certain by the end of this year we will have a full working model of the sales machine in place, and it will be producing the same results as we have seen already in our customer service department. I am convinced we are moving in the right direction to improve sales within our company."

—Jim O'Connell, President of Hotsy Pacific

"We look at business books every hour, every day. *The Machine* was a welcome standout. Soundview votes by a large committee on which books we are going to select as the 30 Best Business Books of the Year. *The Machine* got a unanimous "Yes" vote. That rarely happens."

—Rebecca Clement,
Publisher of Soundview Executive Book Summaries

"Justin stands on the shoulders of a giant and uses the tools of Dr Goldratt's TOC to focus on the effective management of what will be the principal constraint of all businesses sooner or later in the 21st Century. Justin inspires the necessary cultural change within companies—not only entering into a convincing discussion of what to change and why, but also what to change to and how. The energy and stamina required to make such a change should not be underestimated but, provided you have the courage, *The Machine* provides the direction."

—Andrew Jackson, Chief Executive at Triumph Furniture

THE MACHINE

A RADICAL APPROACH TO THE DESIGN OF THE SALES FUNCTION

JUSTIN ROFF-MARSH

GREENLEAF
BOOK GROUP PRESS

Published by Greenleaf Book Group Press
Austin, Texas
www.gbgpress.com
The Machine: A Radical Approach to the Design of the Sales Function

Distributed by Greenleaf Book Group

For ordering information or special discounts for bulk purchases, please contact Greenleaf Book Group at PO Box 91869, Austin, TX 78709, 512.891.6100.
Cover design by Greenleaf Book Group and Kimberly Lance
Typesetting by Ballistix and Ramesh Kumar Pitchai
Author's photograph by SmartShoot.com and Eric Stracke

Publisher's Cataloging Publication Data is available.

Part of the Tree Neutral® program, which offsets the number of trees consumed in the production and printing of this book by taking proactive steps, such as planting trees in direct proportion to the number of trees used: www.treeneutral.com

ISBN: 978-1-62634-224-8

15 16 17 18 19 20   10 9 8 7 6 5 4 3 2
First Edition

Dedicated to
Warren and Sylvia Roff-Marsh
who instilled in me a love of reading

and

Bo Hye Roff-Marsh
who is always the first to read each page I write

Contents

Acknowledgments

I must first thank Ballistix's clients who have had faith in me over the last 20 years (more than has been warranted, on occasion) and who have welcomed my ongoing experiments on their businesses. These clients are among the silent revolutionaries whose stories are told on the following pages.

I thank the team at Ballistix too for diligently taking my ideas and making them work in practice—and for finding creative workarounds when reality failed to yield to my will!

And a big thank you to the late Eliyahu Goldratt and to the entire TOC community who have been early supporters and frequent contributors to sales process engineering.

Note: The names of our silent revolutionaries' organizations have been changed. This enables me to share information about their experiences that would otherwise be confidential.

Introduction

The *Titanic* is sinking: All is not well in sales.

The sales environment in a typical organization—in most every organization, in fact—is seriously dysfunctional. But rather than focusing on the obvious dysfunction, management is busy with incremental improvement initiatives: sales training, sales force automation (technology of various types), or bolt-on lead-generation activities (e.g., outsourced telemarketing, social media activities). Because none of these initiatives address the root cause of the dysfunction, they amount to nothing more than arranging chairs on the deck of the sinking *Titanic*.

And make no mistake—the *Titanic* is sinking!

It's not that sales is getting worse: The issue is that the rest of the organization is getting so much better while sales clings to the same structure, the same management approach, and the same practices that have been in place for the last fifty years.

SILENT REVOLUTIONARIES

In a small number of companies, across three continents, a silent revolution is in progress. These companies (you'll meet some of them in due course) have challenged the most fundamental assumption about how the sales function should be designed. Consequently, they have built sales environments that barely resemble those in their competitors' organizations.

And they've seen *massive* performance improvements! They've seen improvements in the internal operation of sales:

- Field salespeople are spending 100 percent of their time in the field, performing four business-development meetings a day, five days a week.

- Skilled inside sales teams are generating high volumes of sales activity at shockingly low costs.
- Customer commitments are consistently met, administrative work is always done on time, and sales orders appear more frequently and more predictably.

And they've also seen improvements in the relationship between sales and the rest of the organization:

- Hand-off problems between sales and production have been eliminated.
- Marketing works closely with sales to ensure that salespeople are maintained at full utilization—and marketing has recruited the assistance of engineering (and senior management) to ensure that offers are truly compelling.

As I mentioned above, these changes are the consequence of challenging a single assumption about the design of the sales function: the assumption that *sales should be the sole responsibility of autonomous agents.*

Are Things Really That Bad?

Before I reveal the new assumption embraced by these revolutionaries, it's worth exploring the claim that sales is dysfunctional. Are things really that bad?

Consider the goal of the sales function (its reason for existence). It's tempting to resolve that the goal of sales is *to sell.* But, in most organizations, this just doesn't cut it. To pull its weight, the sales function has to *consistently sell all of the organization's production capacity.* This capacity may consist of a traditional plant and equipment, or it may consist of teams of knowledge workers.

Measured against this more meaningful goal, sales consistently fails in most organizations. In recent history, the modern organization's capacity to produce has accelerated past its capacity to sell, and idle machines and production personnel are costing shareholders dearly, month after month and year after year.

Why, then, is sales underperforming? One reason is that salespeople aren't selling. A typical field salesperson performs just two business-development meetings a week. You read it right. Less than 10 percent of a typical salesperson's capacity is allocated to selling. And that figure is pretty standard across industries and across continents.[1]

The majority of a salesperson's day is dedicated to customer service and administrative activities, to solution design and proposal generation, and to prospecting and fulfillment-related tasks.

Let's turn our attention to management. Why has management not fixed this problem? In many organizations, they have tried. Attempts to reallocate salespeople's work have resulted in problems with service quality (the right hand doesn't know what the left is doing). The other alternative is simply to recruit more salespeople, and many firms have tried that too—with interesting results.

Typically, when you add salespeople to an established team, costs go up immediately (easy to predict, right?). But sales don't. In fact, in most cases, sales *never* increase to the level required to justify those additional costs.

The reason is that salespeople *do not* generate the majority of their sales opportunities. Most sales opportunities spring into existence in spite of (not because of) salespeople's prospecting activities. In most organizations, *existing customers* are by far the greatest source of sales opportunities. When management adds salespeople to an existing team, the same pool of sales opportunities is simply distributed across a larger team of salespeople.

But management's problems don't stop here. Salespeople are incredibly difficult to manage—particularly successful ones! You can't *direct* your salespeople as you can production or finance personnel; you can only *coax* them. And *successful* salespeople are both a blessing and a curse. Sure, they generate orders—but at a price. They run roughshod over production and finance personnel, they ignore management directives, and they make frequent references to "their" customers, implying that they can leave and take the organization's goodwill elsewhere—which, to some extent, they probably can.

In summary, then, when we examine sales, we see a critical organizational function that consistently underperforms, that cannot be scaled (economically), that is in regular conflict with other functions, and whose key assets are, in fact, a contingent liability.

The claim that sales is dysfunctional is no exaggeration!

A New Assumption

It's not hard to validate the claim that sales is typically the sole responsibility of autonomous agents. When we employ salespeople, we advise them that they will be held accountable for outcomes, not activities. We pay them commissions (in part or in full) rather than fixed salaries. And we encourage them, in most cases, to manage their territories, their accounts, and their sales opportunities as if they were, well, their own.

It's true that, increasingly, management is attempting to rein in salespeople's autonomy. We ask salespeople to report their activities in the organization's customer relationship management application (CRM).[2] We pay them a mix of salary and commissions. And we at least pay lip service to the notion that these are *company* accounts.

But we forget that, where true opposites are concerned, no compromise is possible. Salespeople can march either to their own drumbeat or to the beat of a central drummer. When faced with the demand to do both, they will always pick the *least bad* option.

When you consider that the entire organization—not just sales—is engineered around the assumption of salesperson autonomy, it's easy to see that salespeople will always choose autonomy. If you doubt this casual assertion, answer these three simple questions:

1. If an important sales opportunity is lost, who is ultimately responsible?
2. If an important customer is dissatisfied, who is ultimately responsible?
3. If an account falls into arrears on its payments, who is ultimately responsible?

The connection between dysfunction and salespeople's autonomy is also easy to spot. Salespeople spend so little time selling because they have so many responsibilities competing for their limited time, because each salesperson is a self-contained sales function.

Salespeople conflict with other functions because, in their world-view, they see only *their* opportunities and *their* accounts. However, other functions (production, engineering, finance) also have limited capacity and are in receipt of competing demands from *multiple* salespeople.

Salespeople conflict with management because there is simply *no place for management* in a typical sales function. If salespeople own their activities and are held accountable only for outcomes (as is so often advertised), there is literally nothing for management to do. *Managing outcomes*, after all, continues to be an oxymoron, no matter how many times you say it![3]

If the assumption that *sales is the sole responsibility of autonomous agents* is the root cause of this dysfunction, it's clearly time for a new assumption. But what should that be?

The good news is that, if we approach this question with a clear head, the answer is oh so obvious.

We discussed that, relative to other organizational functions, sales is sinking fast. What, then, is causing the rapid ascent of these other functions? In particular, what has caused both the productivity and the quality of manufacturing to increase by many orders of magnitude over the last 100 years?

The answer is the division of labor. The division of labor enabled manufacturing to transition from a cottage industry to the modern manufacturing plant. And the division of labor has had the same catalytic effect on project environments (think construction, aerospace, finance, and even marketing). The modern sales environment resembles manufacturing as it used to look more than a century ago.

But that's about to change! The silent revolutionaries have scrutinized sales for evidence that this function is somehow unsuitable for the division of labor. Their search has been fruitless. The new assumption, around which their sales environments have been engineered and on which this book is based, is as simple as it is powerful.

Sales is the responsibility of a centrally coordinated team.

This book shows how this innocent-looking assumption leads logically to a radical new approach to the design and management of the sales function. It will show you how to apply this approach to your organization (irrespective of the size of your firm or the complexity of what you sell), and it will introduce you to a diverse range of organizations that have trodden this path already (our silent revolutionaries).

THE MACHINE

This book likens the result of this new approach—quite unapologetically—to a machine.

This metaphor is apt because, under this new approach, sales becomes the consequence of a number of interrelated processes—rather than the output of a person. Salespeople become a component in a much larger machine (albeit an important component!). And management assumes total responsibility for the design and day-to-day performance of the sales function (managers own sales targets, and they cannot delegate them away).

In this book, I'll explain why sales must be viewed as a machine, rather than as a person. I'll detail how to create a smoothly functioning sales machine—and how to integrate it with the rest of your organization. And I'll counsel you on the (often perilous) transition from your status quo to *The Machine*.

Part 1

THE CASE FOR CHANGE AND
A NEW MODEL

Chapter 1
AFTER THE REVOLUTION

Jennifer retrieves her smart phone from her purse and brings it to life with one authoritative swipe.

Moments later, she's talking to David—her assistant back at head office. "Good meeting," she answers, "you can go ahead and schedule the requirement-discovery meeting. Yep, you can keep talking to Debra. And the opportunity's actually a retrofit . . . let's say 150 grand."

"I'm all over it," David reassures Jennifer as he updates fields in the customer relationship management application (CRM). "So, you'd better hot-tail it over to Tyson Engineering. Phillip left here half an hour ago, so he should be ready for the presentation when you get there."

❉ ❉ ❉ ❉

Jennifer, David, and Phillip all work for James Sanders Group (JSG), a manufacturer of point-of-sale displays and internal fit-outs. JSG is one of our silent revolutionaries.

JSG is an engineering-centric company. They became successful by solving tough problems and building innovative custom installations.

JSG recently suffered a slow leakage in sales. The problem was not that they were suffering at the hands of a large competitor—that's a battle they were well equipped to fight. What was happening was that numerous small competitors (some of them recent market entrants, others offshore manufacturers) were chipping away at their base: winning numerous small jobs, often at crazy margins.

JSG had recognized that this was not a trend they could reverse solely with superior production performance. They knew they needed sales activity—boots on the ground.

That was easier said than done, however. Each time JSG added a salesperson, the new recruit would win a job or two and then become entangled in account management. Before long, account management would become so all-consuming that sales activity would grind to a halt. While this was happening, JSG's competitors were simply sidestepping those complex jobs and focusing on winning the easy contracts.

Initially, JSG looked to *account managers* (as they had taken to calling them) for a solution to the problem. Ultimately, it became clear that this was a process problem, not a people problem.

The snippet of conversation above speaks volumes about the consequences of JSG's revolution. Jennifer is JSG's business-development manager (BDM). And that's the first unusual thing. Although JSG services all of Australia (an area roughly the size of the continental United States), JSG has just one field salesperson. They need only one salesperson because Jennifer is ten times more productive than any of JSG's competitors' salespeople. While a competitor's salesperson averages two sales meetings a week, Jennifer consistently performs twenty.

Another reason JSG has only one field salesperson is the company discovered that a surprising percentage of sales opportunities (particularly repeat purchases) could be handled by a small (but highly efficient) inside sales team. This team finds and pursues simple opportunities, and, from time to time, it stumbles across opportunities that are significant enough to be escalated to David and Jennifer.

David is the key to Jennifer's efficiency. David and Jennifer talk at least four times a day. Like an air traffic controller, David is Jennifer's eyes and ears. He carefully monitors the status of all sales opportunities—freeing Jennifer to focus only on the sales meetings that appear—as if by magic—in Jennifer's smart phone.

David's official title is *business-development coordinator* (BDC). His responsibility is to manage JSG's portfolio of high-value sales opportunities.

He manages each opportunity like a project. He works tirelessly, trying to schedule the next activity in sequence for each. In most (but certainly not all) cases, the next activity is a meeting with Jennifer. And, of course, Jennifer's objective at each meeting will be to *sell* the next activity—generating still more work for David.

David frees Jennifer of the requirement to do anything other than face-to-face business-development meetings. In addition to appointment scheduling, David performs all of the clerical tasks associated with the management of sales opportunities: data entry, reporting, literature fulfillment, expense tracking, and calendar management.

David routes nonadministrative tasks to other specialist resources within JSG. Customer support issues and requests for quotes are routed to customer service representatives. And requirement discovery and solution design become the responsibility of project leaders.

As each task is handed off, David logs the date in the CRM and leaves himself a prompt to follow up prior to the task's expected completion date. In many cases, these tasks are prerequisites for meetings he has already scheduled for Jennifer. It's critical, therefore, that he keep all the parts of this machine working in unison.

Phillip also makes a significant contribution to Jennifer's tremendous efficiency as a project leader. His job is to manage the interface with engineering and production. Prior to each sale, Phillip works closely with Jennifer. She introduces him to clients early in each engagement to discover their requirements and to conceptualize and design solutions.

Solution design is always a collaborative process. Clients have their say, of course: They want Rolls Royce solutions on Toyota budgets. Phillip represents both engineering and production: He must ensure that whatever is specified can be delivered on time and within budget. And it's Jennifer who uses a mixture of hustle and artful diplomacy to close the gap between the two parties.

After the sale, Phillip is responsible for managing the relationship between production and the client. He's on hand to negotiate change requests and to fine-tune the production plan on those occasions when it becomes obvious there's a gap developing between the client's expectations and the direction of the project.

There's no question that Jennifer is busy. Twenty business-development appointments a week is a lot of work. And then there's the travel—a lot of travel!

But the interesting thing is that Jennifer loves working in this environment. There's no stress. She doesn't feel like a juggler with a hundred balls in the air. The clients are happy too. They understand where her responsibilities begin and end, and they always know exactly who to talk to if something appears to be going wrong.

All Jennifer has to do is show up at meetings and talk to people—and she's really good at that. The selling looks after itself.

MANAGEMENT BY NUMBERS

Matthew is one of James Sanders' two sons. He's in charge of operations and sales. Sales wasn't previously under his purview, but it is now. In spite of the fact that the JSG sales function has more moving parts now, it's actually become simpler to manage.

Matthew chairs a weekly sales meeting. The meeting consists of a review of a simple dashboard. The team's primary concern is the size of four critical queues of work. There's a queue of forward-booked meetings in Jennifer's calendar, and there's a queue of sales opportunities upstream from David and from each of the two inside salespeople.

Matthew knows that the profitability of the firm requires a steady flow of work to the plant. He also understands that the primary driver of this flow is the volume of selling conversations performed by his sales team. Any hiccups in sales activity will result in idle machines and workers in a month or so.

Matthew keeps an eye on other indicators too. He scans run charts, looking for unhealthy trends, and scrutinizes cycle times for critical activities to ensure that protective capacities are being maintained.

Matthew's biggest sales challenge is maintaining the support capacity required to keep up with the sales team's unrelenting flow of orders.

Prior to the revolution, Jennifer was one of five account managers. Today, two of those account managers have been converted into project leaders (and one came inside to kick-start the inside sales team). To free project leadership capacity, Matthew has been building a team of customer service representatives, but this team is under the pump too. Every month, it seems like there are a couple of new faces in there.

ARRESTING THE DECLINE

JSG is clearly a different organization today. Sales used to be the responsibility of five overburdened account managers. Now, in place of those account managers, there's a team of specialists. A campaign coordinator ensures that two inside salespeople can have thirty (mostly outbound) selling conversations a day. A percentage of those sales opportunities are escalated to David, who coordinates Jennifer and the team of project leaders. And behind the scenes, a customer service team looks after the processing of orders, the generation of quotations, and the resolution of customer issues.

Today, JSG's sales function is a clearly a machine!

But the impact has not been just on sales. The revolution in sales has benefited most of JSG's other functions too. Sales and engineering work closely together now—to the obvious benefit of both. A full order book has simplified the lives of the production team—they are consistently busy, and they like it that way! And even finance has benefited—the team-based approach to sales eliminated the requirement for sales commissions and, consequently, the requirement for finance to mediate constant disputes over compensation.

As you would expect, these changes have had a profound impact on JSG's profitability. At the beginning of the journey, small increases in operating expense were easily compensated for by additional sales activity. But over time, the gap between revenues and expenses has widened at an increasing rate, thanks to economies of scale in both sales and production.

THEORY INTO PRACTICE

This chapter has shown you the implications of *sales process engineering* (SPE) for one business environment (an engineer-to-order manufacturer).

Chapters 2 and 3 will show you why SPE is so important in today's business environment, introduce you to SPE's four fundamental principles, and then explain how these simple principles lead logically to the end result exemplified by JSG's story.

Chapter 4 will introduce you to the inside-out model: the model most commonly employed by our silent revolutionaries.

One message that will play over and over throughout this book is that you cannot improve the performance of sales by focusing solely on the sales function. This theme will be tackled head-on in chapter 5.

In chapter 6, you'll learn how to apply SPE's principles to create profound improvements in the performance of a range of business environments (including indirect sales and small businesses).

In part 1's final chapter, chapter 7, we'll explore the case for the elimination of salespeople's commissions.

And then, part 2 is dedicated to the practical application of SPE in your organization. It's time to go to work!

Free Video Course: Subscribe Now

Beyond The Machine:
Class 1

Meaningful Selling
Interactions

Presented by: Justin Roff-Marsh
Author: The Machine
Founder: Ballistix

0:00:07   0:13:39

Beyond The Machine is a six-lesson video short course that builds on what you've learned in *The Machine* with intensely practical advice from the trenches.

Subscribe free here: www.beyond-the-machine.com

Chapter 2
FOUR KEY PRINCIPLES

Our first order of business is to address two questions that have the potential to derail this discussion. The issue is not that these questions expose weaknesses in sales process engineering (SPE). The issue is that these questions stand in the way of even being able to start our discussion.

Considering the radical nature of the change we're contemplating, it's only natural to ask these questions: If the traditional sales model is so dysfunctional, and if there's a better method available, why haven't more companies adopted it already? And if the traditional model has withstood the test of time, how can it be that this model is fundamentally flawed?

WHY DO WE PERSIST?

There are two (interrelated) reasons we persist with the traditional approach to the design of the sales function. First, the traditional model conforms to all our assumptions about how sales should be made. Second, it is impossible to inch one's way to the inside-out model; that requires a revolution.

Deeply Held Assumptions

If we are to evaluate the traditional model with reference to enduring and deeply held assumptions about how to generate sales, the traditional approach to the design of the sales function measures up well.

Ask yourself whether you agree with the following statements:

1. Sales of expensive products and services are highly dependent on personal relationships.

2. A successful sales function is highly dependent on *star performers*.

3. Salespeople should be encouraged to operate autonomously—to view their territory almost as if it's their own business.

4. Sales is essentially an *outside* activity.

5. Customers require—and benefit from—a *single point of contact* with their suppliers.

6. Sales improvement is all about improving conversion (plugging the leaky funnel).

Each of these statements sounds innocent enough, right? But, for most salespeople—and their managers—these statements are more than true. They are axioms; they are fundamental, self-evident, and unquestionable truths. Attempts to challenge them will be met with injured feelings—or even hostility.

Consequently, any approach to sales improvement that is in alignment with these axioms will *feel* right, but an approach that conflicts with one or more will almost certainly be dismissed out of hand. As you'll discover in due course, SPE conflicts with every one of these statements—and with numerous other commonly held beliefs about sales too.

Sadly, the serious consideration of SPE tends to require at least one of the following conditions: The performance of the sales function must be so bad as to shake management's faith in the traditional model to its very core, or senior executives with no prior exposure to sales (perhaps an engineering or production specialist) must turn their attention to the sales function and refuse to adopt the existing orthodoxy. Almost without exception, our silent revolutionaries began their investigation of SPE only when *both* of these conditions were in place!

Incremental Change Won't Cut It

The other hurdle to the adoption of SPE is the magnitude of change required for the successful transition. Consider just a few of the changes that have to occur: A significant percentage of the activities associated with the acquisition and maintenance of accounts must be moved inside. Salespeople must willingly give up ownership of calendars, accounts, and even sales opportunities. Field salespeople must be prepared to spend all of their time in the field (in practice, this means a five- to tenfold increase in territory size and, consequently, a lot more travel). Management must be prepared to add new team members and—possibly—to see some existing team members exit the organization. Management must be prepared to assume (and, ultimately, reassign) responsibility for the origination of sales opportunities.

And then there's the impact on the rest of the organization. In pretty much every case, customer service needs to be reengineered to cope with the additional load. Organizational functions must be tightly integrated with one another. New product development must work closely with marketing, and engineering must march in lockstep with both sales and production. If production scheduling has devolved into brinkmanship to accommodate the demands of competing salespeople, scheduling must be fixed, and the master schedule must become sacrosanct.

When you consider the counterintuitive nature of SPE and the significance of the transition from the traditional model, it's no wonder that the traditional model persists.

But it can persist for only so long!

How Did We Get Here?

The traditional sales model hasn't always been dysfunctional. For much of the history of industry, this model has been the optimal one. (In fact, there are situations today in which the traditional model is still quite appropriate.) What has happened is that industry itself has undergone two sea changes, and sales has remained much the same.

Sea Change 1: From Production-Focused to Sales-Focused

In the 1989 film *Field of Dreams*, Kevin Costner's character plows under his corn and builds a baseball field in response to the promise that "if you build it, he will come." Fortunately, Shoeless Joe Jackson and friends arrive just in time to rescue the hapless farmer from bankruptcy.

Today, the phase *build it, and they will come* is often used to reference the unrealistic expectation that production is sufficient to create a market. However, for most of the history of industry, production has, in fact, been sufficient.

Until recently, the salesperson's job was to take a highly differentiated product and demonstrate it to potential customers. Sure, there was a requirement for some salesmanship, but for the most part, the sale was *really* made in new product development and production.

Today, because the market is so much more competitive, it's unusual for a product to be highly differentiated. It's common for customers to choose product A over product B and reasonably expect to pay a similar price for a product that performs almost identically. It's true that we still have true groundbreaking products, but these tend to be the exception rather than the rule.

Because *production* has been the primary success driver for most of our recent history, this is where our capital and our brainpower have been invested. And the return on this investment has been staggering. Over the last hundred years, we've seen massive increases in productivity (measured against any reasonable standard) and improvements of a similar magnitude in quality as well.

We've seen at least three major revolutions in production. Frederick Winslow Taylor introduced scientific management at the start of the last century. Henry Ford's approach to mass production drove costs down to unprecedented levels. And, in the 1950s, W. Edwards Deming jump-started the quality movement, contributing to the rise of Japan, and subsequently revolutionizing operating procedures in production facilities the world over.

Of course, the rate of change we've seen in production cannot be sustained forever. Increasingly, managers are recognizing that their advances in production have exposed sales (including distribution[4]) as the weak link.

Today, sales is the new frontier. We're already seeing the focus of senior management shift to sales—and with focus comes capital and brainpower. My prediction is that the next fifty years will bring revolutions in sales similar in scope and consequence to those we've seen in production.

Let this book be the first shot across the bow of the good ship *Orthodoxy*!

Sea Change 2: From Make to Stock to Engineer to Order

As was mentioned previously, the fundamental assumption that sits at the base of the traditional sales model is that *sales is the sole responsibility of an autonomous agent.* If we consider how a typical organization has been structured for most of the history of industry, this assumption is a perfectly reasonable one.

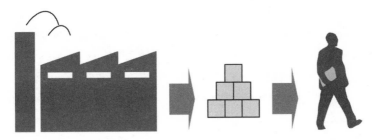

Figure 1. Make to stock.

Figure 1 shows a traditional value chain. The production facility produces to maintain a stockpile of inventory, and the salesperson sells from this inventory.

In this environment, it makes perfect sense for the salesperson to operate autonomously. The firm as a whole benefits when its salespeople sell as much as possible. Because inventory is already sitting in a stockpile, orders can be fulfilled as soon as they are received. And because of this stockpile, minimal interaction is required between sales and production.

Figure 2. Make to order.

Increasingly, this is not how value-chains are configured. We have seen a recent and dramatic shift from *make-to-stock* to *make-to-order* environments, as in figure 2. The latter reduces holdings costs and provides customers with greater choice. In a make-to-order environment, it no longer makes sense for the salesperson to simply sell as much as possible; the salesperson needs to sell only what production has the capacity to produce. Rather than operating autonomously, the salesperson must *subordinate* to production.

This is complicated by a further twist in the value chain. Today, an increasing number of products (as well as almost all services) are actually designed (engineered) as they are being sold. In an *engineer-to-order* environment, tight integration between sales, engineering, and production is critical. The degree of integration determines both the likelihood of the sale being won and the quality of the product delivered.

In such an environment, sales cannot possibly be the sole responsibility of an autonomous agent. In fact, for this reason, the traditional model damages both sales performance and product quality—and, therefore, customer satisfaction.

In summary, the traditional model always has and perhaps always will make sense in make-to-stock environments—where it is possible for the sales function to operate at arm's length from production. Such environments include most consumer goods (typically sold in retail environments), consumer and small-business financial services (insurance and investment products), and packaged software.

However, in make-to-order and particularly in engineer-to-order environments, the requirement for tight integration between sales, engineering, and production renders the traditional model dangerously inappropriate. These environments include business services (consulting, legal, and finance), design-and-construct building, and enterprise software.

Now that we understand why sales environments look the way they do today—and why change is not necessarily an appealing proposition—let's return to the task at hand: redesigning the sales function.

DIRECTION OF THE SOLUTION

Let's consider how we might go about causing a dramatic increase in the productivity of the sales function. What might be the *direction* of the solution?

We should immediately discount traditional sales-improvement initiatives (e.g., sales training or adjustments to the comp plan). History suggests that at best such initiatives produce only incremental results.

For inspiration, we might look to manufacturing. This makes sense because we know that this is one part of the organization that *has* seen a dramatic increase in productivity in recent times.

Do we know the cause of this dramatic change? As it happens, we do.

In 1776, in his magnum opus, *An Inquiry into the Nature and Causes of the Wealth of Nations*, Adam Smith predicted that the division of labor would drive a massive increase in productivity. He told the story of a pin-manufacturing operation in which ten workers had divided the production procedure into eighteen distinct steps and then distributed these steps among themselves.

Individually, each worker could produce twenty pins a day. Collectively, they were producing 48,000!

The benefits of the division of labor are not enjoyed only in manufacturing environments. If we take a stroll around a typical organization, we discover the division of labor in all types of production environments, in engineering, and even in finance. In fact, the only part of the organization that has not embraced the division of labor is sales!

Assuming there is no reason to immediately disqualify the division of labor, let's assume that this is the direction of our solution.

Playing Devil's Advocate

But, not so fast! If we were to commission an experienced salesperson to defend the traditional model—to be the devil's advocate, as it were—can we imagine their objections to the concept of division of labor?

These are likely to be their two primary objections:

1. Complexity. Sales is complex in most environments nowadays. You have multiple influencers and decision makers. You have numerous conversations with multiple parties spanning weeks or months. This complexity does not lend itself to division of labor.
2. Personal relationships. People buy from people. No one likes to transact with a machine. The division of labor will destroy the critical personal relationship between the salesperson and the customer.

Before I directly address these objections, it's interesting to observe that these are similar in nature to the objections you might hear from a craftsperson (an artisan) who is being encouraged to transition to a modern manufacturing environment. This person is likely to suggest that if they do not *personally* craft their product, any increases in efficiency will surely be offset by a reduction in quality.

Of course, history suggests that the artisan's concerns are unwarranted! It just so happens that the changes we must make to a production process to improve efficiency are the very same changes that are required to maximize quality. (In case you're wondering, we improve efficiency, in part, by reducing variability within a production process. And as variability reduces, so does the defect rate.)

Complexity

Our devil's advocate is correct. A modern sales environment is certainly likely to be complex—for all the reasons stated. But is complexity a reason to avoid the division of labor?

If it is, we should see a decline in the division of labor as we examine production environments of increasing complexity. Let's consider two extremes in a production context: the assembly of a hang-glider and the assembly of a jet aircraft. The notion of a single person assembling even the simplest of jet aircraft is laughable. The fact is, in truly complex environments, the division of labor is not just possible; it's essential.

Our devil's advocate has hinted at a potential problem in the application of the division of labor—one we'll grapple with in due course—but he has not dealt our proposed solution a lethal blow.

Personal Relationships

It's true that people enjoy (for the most part) interacting with other people.[5] It's also true that many salespeople have good relationships with their customers. However, it's dangerous to assume (as salespeople frequently infer) that these relationships *cause* sales.

To see why, we should inquire into the origin of a salesperson's relationships. Specifically, which comes first—the sale or the relationship? The reality is, for the most part, that the salesperson's relationships are the *consequence* of sales, not their first cause!

Now, our devil's advocate is unlikely to take this line of reasoning lying down. His immediate objection will surely be that the distinction between first and proximate cause is purely academic—and that if relationships and sales are related, it matters little how they came to be that way.

It's here that we must make a critical distinction—a distinction between the initial transaction in a series of transactions and the rest of those transactions. In most cases, the salesperson's initial transaction signals the acquisition of a new account. All of the subsequent transactions (assuming the same product or service type) are repeat purchases. The first transaction—because it signals the acquisition of an annuity—is many times more valuable than any of the subsequent ones.

Because initial and subsequent transactions are materially different, it doesn't make sense to lump them together and refer to them all as *sales*, as our devil's advocate is doing.

So, for the balance of this book, I will use the word *sale* to refer only to the acquisition of a new account (or the sale of a new product or service line to an existing one). I will refer to repeat transactions as just *transactions*.

We must consider, now, the contribution that the salesperson's relationship makes to the retention of existing accounts. There's no question that this relationship must factor into the *retention* equation, but what are the other considerations?

As we'll discuss in much more detail, every organization must have three core functions to be viable in the long run: new product development, sales, and production. It's revealing to rank these three functions in the order in which we believe they will affect account retention.

Although salespeople all over the world are allocated responsibility for retention, it is extraordinarily rare to find a salesperson who will identify *sales* as the primary influencer of retention. Almost without exception, salespeople recognize that production performance is the primary influence. In other words, the number-one thing an organization must do to retain its customers is deliver on time, in full, without errors.

Salespeople will also willingly volunteer that the number-two thing that an organization must do is ensure that its products are consistently better than—and cheaper than—its competitors', which is, of course, the responsibility of new product development.

The shocking reality is that salespeople contribute little to retention, relative to production and new product development—even though retention is their responsibility.

If you are deficient in the areas of production or new product development, it may be that your salespeople's personal relationships cause accounts to persist with your organization a little longer than they otherwise would. However, to claim that *personal relationships cause sales* amounts to either equivocation or outright denial (or a little of each).[6]

PUTTING THE DIVISION OF LABOR TO WORK: FOUR KEY PRINCIPLES

With those objections out of the way, we've bought ourselves a little bit of time to piece together our solution. The division of labor is not the solution, after all—just the direction of the solution. Our devil's advocate intuitively recognized this when he raised the objection about complexity.

The thing is, when we apply the division of labor to any environment, the situation tends to get a lot worse before it gets better. The rewards offered by the successful transition from the craft shop to the division of labor are exciting (as was reported by Adam Smith all those years ago), but the transition itself is difficult and extraordinarily perilous.

The fact that production has been the primary focus of industry for the last hundred years is evidence of the difficulty of the transition. The good news is that if we intend to lead our sales function down the path already taken by production, this is indeed a well-trodden path.

The lessons from manufacturing can be generalized into four fundamental principles:

1. Scheduling should be centralized.
2. Workflows should be standardized.
3. Resources should be specialized.
4. Management should be formalized.

We'll dedicate the balance of this chapter to the exploration of these principles—in their natural manufacturing context. And in the next chapter we'll figure out how to repurpose these principles for the sales environment. First, however, we need to be sure we understand the nature of the problem we are attempting to solve. To achieve that, we'll turn our attention to a boat race.

The Primary Challenge

In fact, let's consider two boat races—both of them time trials. In each case, the oarsmen will attempt to maximize the speed of their vessels. (In the first race, the oarsmens' times will be averaged to determine the result.)

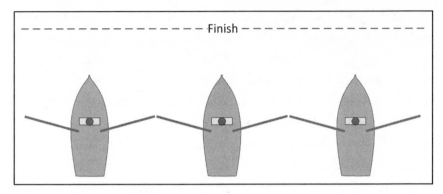

Figure 3. Autonomous agents.

In the first race, each oarsman commandeers his own boat. Each is an autonomous agent. When the starter's gun fires, each oarsman must do his level best to maximize the speed of his vessel. And he does that, not surprisingly, by rowing as fast as is humanly possible. This race is an allegory for the *craft shop* environment in manufacturing and for the traditional sales model.

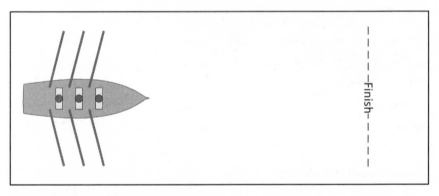

Figure 4. Division of labor.

In the second race, we make one subtle change. We put all the oarsmen in one boat. The goal is the same: to reach the finish line in the shortest amount of time. But each of the oarsmen must undergo a radical shift in his approach to the goal. If each oarsman rows as fast as possible, the speed of the vessel will definitely not be maximized.

If each oarsman maximizes his individual rate of work, the consequences will be a lot of noise, clashing of oars, and, possibly, a capsized boat. In this second race (an example, of course, of the division of labor), the speed of the vessel is determined primarily by the *synchronization* of the oarsmen—not by their individual rates of work.

Now, the shift of focus from individual effort to synchronization may not seem significant, but it is—particularly when we consider environments more complex than a rowboat. Learning to row in unison with others is tricky, but this skill (in this context) is made easier by the fact that you are operating in close proximity to your colleagues (you stroke in time with the person in front of you), and the fact that you have immediate feedback (you can see and feel the impact of your actions on the performance of the vessel).

This tends not to be the case in a typical work environment (few people, today, work in rowboats).

In a reasonable-sized manufacturing plant, for example, it's unlikely that all of the workers contributing to a process are in visual contact with one another. And, in a knowledge-work environment, such as—say—a sales function, work in progress is invisible, and lead times are long—meaning that there is no immediate feedback.

In such an environment, how do workers synchronize their rates of work? The short answer is that, without special intervention, *they simply don't.*

Here's an interesting thought experiment:

Consider the changes we would need to make to our rowboat model in order for this model to be representative of a standard knowledge-work environment.

How about we replace each of the oarsmen with a rowing machine—a powerful solenoid, operated by remote control? And let's put each of our oarsmen in a cubicle in an office complex, and equip each with a remote control unit. On each remote control unit is a button that actuates the solenoid back in the boat and causes that oarsman's two oars to stroke.

If each oarsman is isolated from the boat—and from his colleagues—and he is committed to winning that race, how will he determine when to press the button?

Sadly, this scenario is not dissimilar to many modern work environments. To complete the picture, all we need to do is add a manager who attempts to improve the performance of the boat by running from cubicle to cubicle encouraging everyone to row harder—and then who periodically berates team members for their lack of communication.

Principle 1: Scheduling Should Be Centralized

To claim that the division of labor causes workers to become disconnected from the performance of their overall system is stating the obvious. After all, as we'll soon discuss, a narrowing of the worker's focus is both a benefit of and a necessary condition for the division of labor.

It's inevitable, then, that the division of labor will result in synchronization problems.[7] The solution is to centralize scheduling.

Any work you perform can be broken into two components. The first of these are the critical activities that cause matter (or information) to change the form, sequence, and timing of each of these activities.

The second component is what I'll be referring to as *scheduling*. Of course, scheduling is pretty easy when it's just you doing the work. You can learn the basics in a half-day time-management workshop. However, as you add more workers to the work environment, scheduling rapidly becomes more complex.

The key to avoiding synchronization problems when we apply the division of labor is to first split the responsibility for these two components of work. If we fail to do this, the local efficiency improvements that result from workers focusing on a single task will quickly be eaten up by the general chaos that spreads through the environment—like those clashing oars in the rowboat.

There are many environments in which the centralization of scheduling is a well-established practice: the manufacturing plant (in which scheduling is the responsibility of the master scheduler); the project environment (in which the project manager owns the schedule); the orchestra (in a string quartet, the first violin sets the tempo, while in the case of a full orchestra, a dedicated conductor is required); and the airport (consider the chaos if, in the absence of an air-traffic controller, pilots had to decide among themselves when to take off and land!). In each of these cases, scheduling is a specialty.

(The project manager doesn't wear a tool belt, and an air-traffic controller can be quite capable even if they have never flown a plane.)

Now, it's true that even the most complex sales environments are less complex than a busy airport, but it's also true that almost every sales environment is significantly more complex than a rowboat. Therefore, if we are entertaining the idea of applying division of labor to sales, we must first acknowledge that the very first activity for which the salesperson relinquishes responsibility will be scheduling.

Postscript

Until now, we have accepted that, in a simple environment—like a rowboat—the division of labor doesn't require the centralization of scheduling. However, it's interesting to consider what we might do if we were really serious about winning the boat race we discussed earlier. If you look at most competitive rowing teams, you'll discover—you guessed it—centralized scheduling!

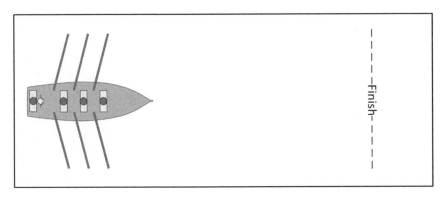

Figure 5. Centralized scheduling.

In a scull, for example, the coxswain sits in the stern of the boat, facing the oarsmen, and sets the tempo to which the oarsmen row. If we consider the racing scull for a moment, we can draw two interesting observations that relate to scheduling in all environments.

First, the coxswain is a dead weight (he does not row), and his inclusion increases the weight of the vessel by a significant amount. It's reasonable to assume, then, that the performance improvement resulting from the inclusion of the coxswain more than compensates for this weight increase. And this is in a simple environment in which the centralization of scheduling is not even critical.

Second, the coxswain maximizes the speed of the boat by causing all of the oarsmen to row at the same speed as the *slowest* oarsman. Therefore, to maximize the speed of the boat, all but one of the oarsmen must row *slower* than their maximum capability.

Principle 2: Workflows Should Be Standardized

The need to standardize all workflows is regarded as self-evident by many managers. Note the attention paid to *standard operating procedures* in the modern workplace. But it's worth acknowledging that standardization is only a necessity in an environment in which the division of labor has been applied.

Interestingly, you can see evidence of this if you look at customer relationship management (CRM) implementations in sales environments. Almost every mid- to large-sized organization has invested tens (or, more commonly, hundreds) of thousands of dollars in this technology in recent years in anticipation of increased sales performance. Few, however, can point to any performance improvement that can be attributed to the CRM.

If you examine business cases for typical CRM implementations, you'll discover that many promises hinge on an assumption that the standardization of salespeople's procedures will cause an increase in sales. Absent the division of labor, this is not a surety. Capable salespeople neither need nor benefit from the standardization of their operating procedures. Consequently, the CRM adds overhead (the additional data entry associated with enforcing standards) without generating any performance uplift.

But the division of labor changes things: Standardization suddenly becomes critical.

When the person who plans the work (the scheduler) is remote from the people who do the work, the standardization of procedures (and workflows) prevents the complexity of environments from multiplying to unmanageable levels.

In manufacturing environments, the workflow is referred to as the *routing*. The routing is the path that work will follow through the plant, taking into account both the activities that will be performed and the resources that will perform them. The general rule in manufacturing is that for production of the same product, the same routing should be followed.

If we apply the division of labor to the sales environment, we must standardize our workflows for the same reason. For this environment to be manageable and scalable, all opportunities of the same type (i.e., the same objective) must be prosecuted using the same routing—from the origination of those opportunities, through their management.

Principle 3: Resources Should Be Specialized

In discussing the centralization of scheduling, we've already broached the subject of specialization. We know that when we apply the division of labor, the scheduler is the very first specialist. Indeed, once we have centralized scheduling and standardized workflows, specialization is relatively easy.

Specialization causes a significant increase in workers' productivity for two reasons: First, when a worker performs activities of just one type, they become very good at performing those activities. Second, switching between materially different activities imposes a significant overhead on a worker. The elimination of this switching (multitasking) increases that worker's effective capacity.

Of course, specialization doesn't relate just to people. In most environments today, activities will be shared between people and machines (including computers). However, we should note that automation has *not* been the root cause of productivity improvement in the last hundred years. The primary cause is the division of labor. After all, it's the division of labor that has allowed us to simplify activities to the point at which they can be performed by machines.

When it comes to dividing activities, it tends to make sense to make divisions along three axes:

1. Location. You should split field and inside activities—meaning that people work inside or outside but never a mix.

2. Work type. You should split activities that are different enough to impose a *switching cost*. For example, creative activities do not mix well with more transactional ones.

3. Cadence. You should split long and short lead-time activities. For example, in a technology environment, you should not mix true development work with break-fix tasks.

Principle 4: Management Should Be Formalized

It's interesting to note that the very first manager was a scheduler (as per our coxswain example). However, as environments grow, so do the responsibilities of management. Today, it's more likely that the manager of a function delegates scheduling to a technical specialist and focuses on the internal performance of their function—as well as its integration with the rest of the organization.

This broader focus makes sense for two reasons: The division of labor causes work environments to become inherently fragile, and because the organization consists of a number of functions—each of which could be characterized as an oarsman in a larger boat—someone must pay attention to the synchronization of the organization as a whole.

Specialization is a two-edged sword. It causes a dramatic increase in the productivity of each individual, but it also causes each worker to operate in a vacuum—intently focused on their own work in progress (their task list). To a great extent, the scheduler compensates for this narrow focus, but the manager is still required to ensure compliance with the schedule, to resolve problems as they occur, and to make decisions relating to the design and resourcing of the overall environment.

Now, the word *formalize* in this fourth principle may seem redundant. After all, in our production example, there was no need for management prior to the division of labor. Why then do we need to formalize management—as opposed to simply adding a manager?

This is one area in which the sales environment differs from our production example. The modern sales function has grown large enough that there is a requirement for a manager to attend to those second-order management responsibilities.

This means that most sales functions have managers—in spite of the fact that they are still essentially craft shop environments. These managers, however, have no understanding of scheduling and no experience managing the kind of environment that will exist after the transition to divided labor.

Accordingly, we will definitely need to convince our sales managers to adopt a more formal approach to management.

Chapter 3
REIMAGINING THE SALES FUNCTION

In this chapter, we'll reason from first principles to the sales function we discovered in chapter 1. Then in the following chapter, we'll expand our discussion to include environments where not all opportunities are major ones—and introduce you to the critical inside sales function.

We commence with the direction of the solution (the division of labor) and our four key principles.

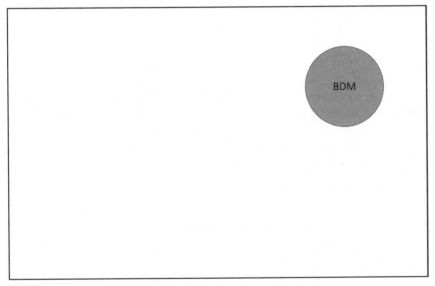

Figure 6. Yesterday's sales function. The business-development manager (BDM).

Yesterday, our sales function essentially consisted of a single salesperson. Tomorrow, sales will be the responsibility of a tightly synchronized team.

Principle 1: Scheduling Should Be Centralized

Our first principle dictates that, as we push toward the division of labor, our very first specialist must be a scheduler. We'll elect to call our scheduler a *business-development coordinator* (BDC). We'll also refer to our salesperson as a *business-development manager* (BDM), to highlight their new focus.

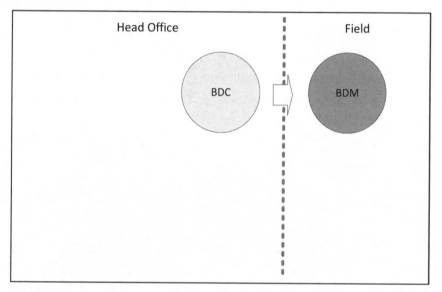

Figure 7. Division of labor, step 1: The business-development coordinator (BDC).

It's important to note that the BDC is *not* a sales assistant. The word *assistant* would imply that it's the BDM who allocates work. The opposite—as is indicated by the direction of the arrow in figure 7—is the case. The BDC pushes work to the BDM.

This means that the BDM must transfer any and all scheduling responsibilities to the BDC. This may be a more significant undertaking than it sounds when you consider that, in most cases, the BDM's scheduling responsibilities are not limited to the management of their own calendar. In most cases, salespeople are interfacing with production and customer service, coordinating the delivery of clients' jobs.

At this point in the discussion, it's premature to allocate specific activities to resources, but it will do no harm to draw four very general conclusions:

1. Our BDC must perform all scheduling.
2. Our BDM will spend more time selling.
3. Our BDM should work in the field (not in an office).
4. Our BDC should work from the head office (ideally—not a regional office).

The first two conclusions are not at all contentious, but the importance of the second two is less obvious.

BDMs Work in the Field, Not in an Office

Traditionally, salespeople split their time between the field and an office. And this is unavoidable when you consider the diverse range of activities for which they are responsible. If we have a choice, however (and we soon will), it makes sense to have BDMs spend all of their time in the field, for two reasons: First, if we are going to spend the (not insignificant amount of) money required to employ enterprise-class salespeople, it makes sense to have them selling in the field, where—presumably—they're more effective. And second, a fundamentally different approach is required for scheduling field- and office-based activities—meaning that it's impractical to schedule a combination of the two.

The BDC Works from the Head Office

It would be tempting to assume that the BDC should operate in close proximity to the BDM—but the opposite is true. The BDC should operate in close proximity to the business functions with which sales must integrate.

We've already discussed that the integration of sales, engineering, and production is increasingly important for the modern organization. Well, that integration is significantly easier to achieve if the individuals responsible for scheduling each function operate in close proximity to one another.

In addition, if you consider the BDM's perspective, the BDM will feel less disconnected from the organization as a whole if their BDC is located in the head office.

The Relationship between the BDC and the BDM

Let's consider the relationship between the BDC and the BDM by contrasting sales with another environment in which we have senior people working closely with schedulers.

That environment is the executive suite. In the executive suite of a decent-size firm, we will likely encounter at least one executive who works closely with an *executive assistant*. Unlike a typical assistant, an *executive* assistant assumes overall responsibility for the initiatives in which the executive is involved—and also assumes responsibility for the executive's calendar.

The executive assistant maintains an awareness of all the initiatives on which the executive is working (and their relative importance) and plans the executive's time so as to maximize the yield on their limited capacity.

If we take the preceding sentence and substitute business-development coordinator for executive assistant and business-development manager for executive, we have a perfect functional description of the role of the BDC. And if we reflect on the nature of the relationship between the executive assistant and the executive, we will observe exactly the relationship that must exist between the BDC and the BDM in order for the sales function to be productive.

This discussion also sheds light on the inevitable questions about, in practice, whether BDMs will find it demeaning for someone else to plan their calendars, and whether potential customers will find it disturbing if BDMs fail to set their own appointments.

The answer to both questions is a firm *no*. Treating salespeople like executives does not demean salespeople; if anything, it elevates their standing in the eyes of potential customers.

The Economics of the BDM–BDC Relationship

At first glance, it would appear that we're multiplying expenses by partnering BDMs with BDCs. Nothing could be further from the truth. A traditional field salesperson averages two face-to-face business-development meetings per week. If you partner that same salesperson with a capable BDC, their effective capacity increases to four meetings per day, or twenty a week. That's a tenfold increase in effective capacity. This means that two BDMs partnered with BDCs will do the same volume of work that would otherwise require ten BDMs working alone.

In practice, this means that you can reduce the size of your team of BDMs (retaining the most capable ones) and still perform the same volume of face-to-face meetings. When you consider that BDCs cost roughly half what BDMs do, the economic benefits are compelling.

PRINCIPLE 2: WORKFLOWS SHOULD BE STANDARDIZED

Our second principle dictates that we use a standard sequence of activities to originate opportunities (i.e., to identify or generate sales opportunities) and to prosecute opportunities (i.e., to pursue them to their ultimate conclusion—either a win or a loss).

Although these two workflows are clearly part of the one value chain, it makes sense to treat them separately, simply because opportunities can be originated in batches; but they must be carried out, or prosecuted, one at a time. Because opportunities can be originated in batches (e.g., via promotional campaigns), the idea of standardizing the first workflow is not particularly contentious. However, the case for standardization is not so clear where opportunity management is concerned. To frame this consideration as a question, do our salespeople require unlimited degrees of freedom in order to effectively win orders?

The Case for Standardization

To address this question, we should first acknowledge that whenever we are selling, a potential customer is buying. Therefore, our opportunity-management workflow is the flip side of our potential customer's procurement workflow. So we can reframe our question as the following: Do our customers require unlimited degrees of freedom in order to make an effective purchasing decision?

Viewed from this perspective, the answer is *not necessarily*. Increasingly, organizations are standardizing their procurement procedures for those products or services they purchase regularly. What's more, different organizations' procurement procedures for comparable products tend to be remarkably similar.

If we consider major purchases, I suspect the greater variation we see in procurement procedures is more a consequence of an absence of procedure than it is evidence of the absence of a need for one. In other words, I'm suggesting that there probably is an objective ideal procedure for making major purchases of various types—it's just that because organizations make major purchases infrequently, they haven't yet determined what that procedure is.

I've often asked groups of salespeople who sell major products (e.g., enterprise software) whether there's a right way and a wrong way for organizations to purchase a product like theirs, and I've always been impressed by how well reasoned (and unanimous) the salespeople's responses are.

My suggestion, then, is that there is an ideal opportunity-prosecution workflow for both minor and major purchases. Where minor purchases are concerned, this is more likely to be determined in advance by your customers, and enormous variation from customer to customer is unlikely. Where major purchases are concerned, there is still an optimal procurement procedure; it's just that customers are unlikely to be aware of it, which presents your salespeople with the opportunity to take the lead and help the customer buy more effectively.

Making It Scalable

Practically, as was mentioned in the previous chapter, the benefits of standardization (in and of itself) are relatively limited. The real value of standardization is that it enables hand-offs between stakeholders in both the sales environment and the associated functions (e.g., engineering and production). Of course, without hand-offs, there can be no division of labor.

Consider the communication between a BDM and a BDC. If an opportunity is being prosecuted according to a preexisting workflow, after each field activity, the BDM needs only to update their BDC with one of four possible next steps. They will recommend:

1. abandoning the opportunity,
2. repeating the activity just performed,
3. scheduling the next activity in sequence, or
4. scheduling an activity further downstream in the workflow.

If the workflow is sensibly constructed, these four options provide sufficient flexibility for both parties, and if more flexibility is required, the design of the workflow should be revised.

The important point, though, is that this structure enables a lot of information to be transferred in just a few words. In designing a workflow, we're not trying to map the existing complexity; rather, we're *engineering it out* of the sales environment (at least to the degree that it's realistic to do so).

Typical Sales Workflows

From a high level, most sales workflows look something like figure 8.

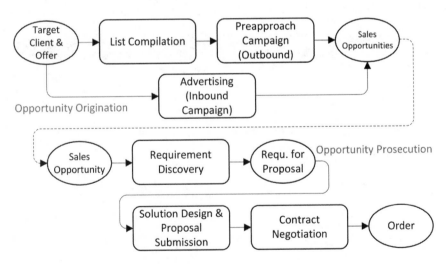

Figure 8. A typical sales workflow.

Although all promotional activities are outbound to some extent, it is convenient to divide promotional campaigns into two categories: *outbound,* in which you assume a requirement and deem there to be a sales opportunity, and *inbound,* in which you engage in advertising (and similar) activities, with a view to generating (inbound) expressions of interest.

Principle 3: Resources Should Be Specialized

If we return to our project analogy for a moment, we now have a project plan (our standard workflow for originating and prosecuting sales opportunities), a project manager (our BDC), and a resource pool containing a single resource (our BDM).

To exploit the benefits of the division of labor, it's now necessary to add some more people to our resource pool. An obvious starting point is to list the activities performed by a typical salesperson (as in table 1) and to determine which are critical for our BDM to perform and which can be allocated to other resources.

Table 1. Activities typically performed by salespeople in the field.

Activity name	Activity type
Prospecting	Promotion
Appointment-setting calls	Administrative
Calendaring and travel arrangements	Administrative
Sales meetings	Sales
Follow-up calls	Administrative
Solution design	Technical
Proposal generation	Semitechnical
Production-related activities	Technical
Postsale customer service	Semitechnical
Processing (repeat) transactions	Semitechnical
Data entry and reporting	Administrative

Beside each activity in table 1 is a proposed activity type. Some of these are obvious, and some are a little contentious, so let's be sure to resolve the contention, if we can, before we reallocate some of these activities:

1. promotion (i.e., the origination of sales opportunities),
2. administration (i.e., critical supporting activities),
3. sales (i.e., meaningful selling conversations),
4. technical (i.e., requirement discovery and solution design), and
5. semitechnical (i.e., quoting, order processing, and issue management).

Promotion

It is possible for salespeople to originate their own sales opportunities, but the fact that they *can* does not constitute an argument that they *should* (and this statement applies to almost every other activity above too). The thing is, the origination of sales opportunities is extremely resource intensive if they are originated one at a time—and salespeople lack the resources required to originate them in batches.

Typically, the batch origination of sales opportunities requires the ability to procure and manipulate contact lists, the ability to produce hard-hitting promotional campaigns, the resources to broadcast personalized email (or snail mail), and perhaps even the ability to promote and coordinate events.

Salespeople lack these capabilities, so it makes sense—at least notionally—to allocate responsibility for opportunity origination to the marketing department. Within the marketing department, the origination of sales opportunities is referred to as *promotion* (one of the four Ps of marketing).

I say that the origination of opportunities is *notionally* the responsibility of marketing because, in practice, the requirement for tight integration between promotion and sales is so strong that the responsibility for the former cannot possibly be delegated (at least in full) to another department.

The practical solution is to add a *campaign coordinator* to sales. This person must be physically located within the sales department because they must be tuned in to the telephone conversations that are occurring as a direct consequence of the campaigns they are coordinating.

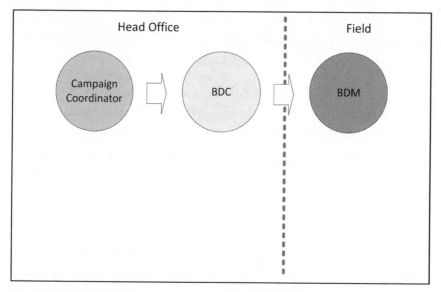

Figure 9. Division of labor, step 2: The campaign coordinator.

It's helpful to think of the campaign coordinator as a member of the marketing department who's on permanent loan to sales. Your campaign coordinator must understand promotional processes and must have good connections to people in your marketing department. But their primary allegiance must be to sales. As we'll see in part 2, your organization's sales activity will quickly grind to a halt if your campaign coordinator loses focus for just a day or so.

The campaign coordinator's reason for existence is very simple: to maintain a queue with an optimal number of sales opportunities upstream from the BDC. This ensures that the BDC always has someone to call when an empty slot appears in the BDM's calendar.

Administrative Tasks

It should be easy to see why data entry, reporting, calendar management, and travel arrangements have been categorized as administrative activities, but what about appointment setting and follow-up calls? How can they possibly be administrative activities?

Let's start with follow-up calls.

As we have discussed already, at each meeting within the opportunity-prosecution workflow, it's the BDM's job to sell the next critical activity in the workflow. If the BDM has done their job properly, the scheduling of that activity is purely an administrative function.

On the occasion when a BDC discovers that further input from the BDM is required before the next activity in the workflow can be scheduled, the BDC should schedule either another meeting with the salesperson or a conference call. In either case, this additional meeting does not constitute a material change to the opportunity-prosecution workflow; it's just a repeat of the last performed activity.

If you think about it, the initial appointment-setting call is no different from follow-up calls. If the initial meeting has already been sold, the call is simply a scheduling exercise.

Consider this real-world example:

Nigel is the director of sales for a large recruitment firm (one of our silent revolutionaries). Because he also happens to be the most capable public speaker in the sales department, he's now addressing a room full of senior executives, introducing a controversial approach to headcount management.

At the close of his presentation, he will ask the delegates to complete a feedback form and will encourage them to tick a box at the bottom of the form to indicate they would like to schedule a best-practices briefing with Rick, the firm's local consultant (salesperson).

It's Nigel's expectation that a little more than 20 percent of the delegates will tick that box, and that virtually all of those will meet with Rick. What's interesting is that Rick's BDC is unlikely to call any of them. Setting those appointments is such a simple undertaking that she will simply send each an email, asking them to indicate their preference from a number of available meeting slots in Rick's calendar.

In this case, it's clear that the *initial* appointment-setting call is purely administrative in nature. Of course, this is in contrast to the status quo—in which the initial appointment-setting call is most definitely a sales call.

A major benefit of classifying the initial appointment-setting call as administrative in nature is that it forces you to sell the meeting in advance of the call. This is hugely beneficial, because it highlights the difficulties that BDCs might have setting meetings and it forces management to create more compelling offers and market propositions. In turn, the more compelling offers (and market propositions) result in better-quality appointments, and that benefits everyone.

Of course, the origination of sales opportunities is a challenging subject, one we'll return to in part 2 of the book.

Technical Tasks

Every engineer-to-order environment has the same problem. Salespeople become entangled in the delivery of the solutions they sell—and this entanglement cannibalizes their selling capacity (and generates a host of other problems). This inevitable entanglement has a simple cause.

The thing is, above a certain level of product complexity, a perfect hand-off from sales to production is impossible. It's not just difficult; it's *impossible*. This means that beyond this *complexity threshold*, information will always be lost when sales hands off a project to production. This information loss cannot be eliminated with more detailed briefings, more documentation, or management exhortations to communicate better.

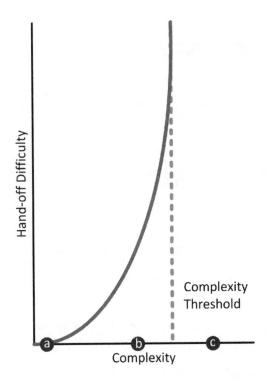

Figure 10. This graphical depiction of the complexity threshold shows that hand-off difficulty goes to infinity when complexity increases beyond a certain point. The markers on the x-axis suggest the degree of complexity in three environments: (a) make to stock (b) make to order and (c) engineer to order.

There are only two possible solutions to this problem: We can propose only products that are simple enough to sit beneath the complexity threshold (e.g., limit customization to a fixed menu of options), or we can eliminate the requirement for a hand-off altogether.

Of course, in major-sales environments, the second option tends to be the default approach. What happens is that the salesperson never fully hands off to production; they remain on-call, after the sale, to answer questions and to interface with the client.

There is, however, another approach, one that has a profound impact on both the effectiveness of sales and service quality. The alternative approach is to add a third party to the mix, a person we'll call a *project leader*.

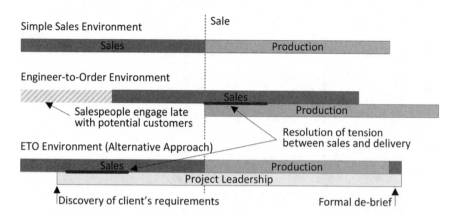

Figure 11. In a major-sales environment there are two approaches to the avoidance of hand-offs. In the default approach, the salesperson remains engaged through delivery. This results in a reduction in the salesperson's selling capacity and, consequently, late engagement with potential clients. It also defers resolution of the inevitable tension between sales and production until after the sale is won.

In this alternative approach, the project leader and the BDM work side by side for most of the opportunity-prosecution workflow.

Here are the essential characteristics of this approach: Because the BDM has no postsale responsibilities, they have more selling capacity. This enables them to engage earlier with clients than they otherwise would—meaning that initial contacts are conceptual in nature. At the point at which the client wishes to discuss (in concrete terms) their requirements, the BDM introduces the project leader. The project leader takes responsibility for *requirement discovery* and for *solution design* (in many cases, these will occur in the form of a formal solution-design workshop). From this point until the point of sale, the BDM and the project leader work together. The project leader is responsible for the technical component of the engagement, and the salesperson tends to the commercial component. After the sale, the project leader champions the project as it moves through production. This means that the project leader replaces the BDM as the primary point of contact for both production and the client.

The sole responsibility of the project leader is to manage the interface between production and both the client and sales. When they do their job well, the product presented to the client is both salable and deliverable (taking into account, for example, features, price, delivery lead time), and the product that is ultimately delivered to the client fulfills the client's requirements, without compromising the profitability of the organization (understanding that the client's requirements may well have changed—or been reinterpreted—during delivery).

Because the project leader seeks to optimize the numerous trade-offs though both the opportunity-management and delivery phases of the engagement, it should be clear that their role is critical and their contribution invaluable. For this reason, the project leader should always have protective capacity; they should never be overburdened with work. Accordingly, it is *not* a problem that the project leader works both in the office and in the field. If we are deliberately maintaining the project leader at less than 100-percent utilization, it is obviously not necessary to maximize their efficiency.

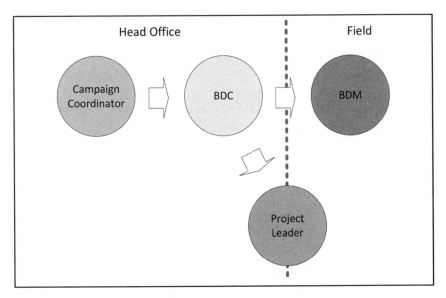

Figure 12. Division of labor, step 3: The project leader.

Semitechnical Tasks

Semitechnical activities include the generation of standard proposals, the processing of repeat transactions, and the provision of after-sales support (e.g., issue resolution). All these activities—as well as any others that are semitechnical in nature—should be allocated to the customer service team.

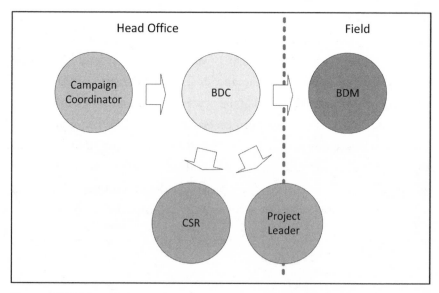

Figure 13. Division of labor, step 4: Customer service representatives.

Although most organizations already have customer service teams, the primary responsibility for customer service rests with the salesperson. The result tends to be that the customer service representatives (CSRs) are disillusioned and generally unprepared to take ownership of customer service cases (I'll use the word *case* to refer to a unit of customer service work).

This means that two changes must occur: The customer service team must rapidly develop both the capability and the capacity to take full ownership of the entire customer service caseload, and salespeople must extricate themselves from customer service. In practice, the latter is not as difficult as it sounds. With two simple initiatives, it can be accomplished quite quickly:

First, salespeople must avoid taking ownership of customer service cases in the first instance. This is easier than it sounds. For example, if a customer asks a question about an incorrect order, the salesperson might use their cell phone to initiate a three-way conference call between the customer, a CSR, and themselves.

Second, customer service representatives must *assume* ownership of cases as soon as they encounter them. With this in mind, it is useful, in the design of your customer service workflow, to stipulate that the CSR must send the client an email when each case is opened and closed. Obviously, the first email should make it clear that the CSR is the person responsible for resolving the issue and is, consequently, the primary point of contact.

The customer service team must be close to production, ideally, in the same building. If there's a requirement to perform field visits in order to resolve customer service cases (perhaps to inspect a problematic product), the CSR should task the project leader to perform this visit and report back with necessary information.

If we return to our project analogy—in which I compared a BDC with a project manager—we can now see that our BDC has inherited a resource pool consisting of three resources (salesperson, project leader, and CSR). This means that in order to prosecute each sales opportunity, the BDC will break the opportunity into a series of activities and allocate each activity to one or more of these resources, in accordance with the routing specified in the opportunity-prosecution workflow.

The Customer's Perspective

It's easy to see that this model is quite ordered and logical from the organization's perspective, but what about the customer? In asking our customers to interface with multiple people, haven't we just made their world more complex?

It's true that in this model, customers will interface with four people (BDC, salesperson, project leader, and CSR). It's also true that, today, most customers ask for—and most organizations strive to provide—a single point of contact. However, reality is a little more complicated than this.

It's a mistake to commence this discussion with an assumption that the traditional model delivers good customer service. It simply doesn't. It's also a mistake to take at face value customers' claims that they'd rather have a single point of contact. In practice, customers can be quite aggressive in seeking out relationships with other individuals if they sense that this is in their best interest.

My experience is that the following statements are closer to the truth (particularly in major-sales environments): What customers really want is a *single conversation*. In other words, they will willingly speak with multiple people within your firm, as long as they do not have to repeat themselves. If customers have a choice between dealing with a single generalist and multiple specialists, they would rather speak with specialists. Although we talk about *the customer* as if this were a single entity, in most cases, there are multiple people on the customer side involved in the purchase and consumption of your products.

You will discover that this new model provides a vastly better quality of service, provided you ensure that there is a clear delineation of the responsibilities of the various parties with whom customers interact and that BDCs (who plan all opportunity-management activities) and CSRs (who tend to become customers' primary points of contact between projects) remain in close communication with one another.

PRINCIPLE 4: MANAGEMENT SHOULD BE FORMALIZED

As we discussed, the downside of the division of labor is that it causes environments to become fragile. Although it's the responsibility of the BDC to synchronize the various team members, management oversight is critical for a number of reasons. BDCs tend to be younger and less experienced than both BDMs and project leaders. Accordingly, the BDC's mandate is very limited. If the sales environment is operating exactly as it should be, they have total control over the schedule. However, a relatively small disturbance in the operation of the environment can render them impotent. The sales function must integrate effectively with other functions (production and marketing, to name two). Because the BDC tends to be relatively inward looking, it's necessary for a more senior person to interface with those other departments. In most sales environments, there are multiple BDCs (one for each salesperson). This means that a more senior person must manage any contention between BDCs (or BDMs).

In most environments, there's actually a requirement for two managers. You'll need a supervisor to oversee the internal team and a more senior person to manage the overall sales environment (including field operators). How exactly to resource these two management requirements is a sensitive subject (particularly in smaller businesses), so we'll have to defer this discussion until part 2 of the book.

❄ ❄ ❄ ❄

In chapter 1, we encountered James Sanders Group (JSG—one of our silent revolutionaries). We discussed Jennifer's enormous productivity and the productive relationship she has with David (her BDC) and Phillip (a project leader). We also discussed the critical role that customer service has played in the remarkable transition that has occurred at JSG.

In this chapter, we have seen how the four key principles guide us logically to JSG's sales model—or, at least, to the more intriguing elements of JSG's model. However, in the interests of simplicity, we have sidestepped a discussion of what's arguably the most important element of JSG's model: *inside sales*.

Chapter 4
THE DEATH OF FIELD SALES

This discussion is worthy of its own chapter for a couple of reasons. First, as you're about to discover, the odds are pretty good that *you* need an inside sales team. And, what's more, the creation of this team should probably take priority over whatever changes you plan to make to your outside sales activities. And, second, our discussion of inside sales is going to bring us face to face with a set of fundamental changes in the way most markets function. And that's not a bad place to start.

As I write this, "The Death of Field Sales" is my most popular lecture topic. Most event organizers assume that I exaggerate in order to capture the attention of busy executives. Well, it's true that headlines often benefit from a little hyperbole, but there's less exaggeration here than you might expect. In most markets, either field sales is dying or it's already dead.

Of course, I'm not heralding the end of field salespeople. There is a requirement for field salespeople in some (but definitely not all) markets now—and there will always be circumstances in which face-to-face selling is indispensable. On their way to extinction are environments in which sales is *essentially* an outside activity. Even in engineer-to-order environments today (think JSG), only a tiny percentage of the total volume of activities required to originate and prosecute a sales opportunity are performed in the field. And those important field activities would simply not occur if it were not for the volume of work performed inside.

The fact is, sales today is an inside endeavor, supported, in some cases, with discrete field activities.

If you want proof, follow one of your field salespeople around for a week. What you're likely to discover is that your field salesperson spends less than 10 percent of their time in the field. The balance of their time will be spent in an office of some kind (your head office, a branch office, a home office, or a makeshift office in the backseat of a rental car). If my prediction is correct, you'll probably conclude that your salesperson is not really a field salesperson at all. They are an inside salesperson who performs occasional field activities.

There are still some markets in which sales is essentially an outside activity—trade tools, for example. Think of Snap-on, whose operators pilot their white, red, and black trucks directly to workshops and building sites and sell on the spot. But these markets are the exception, not the rule. It's rare today to find customers who are happy for salespeople to drop in unannounced. Actually, in addition to making drop-ins impossible, most organizations go to quite some effort to rebuff even those salespeople who are polite enough to attempt to schedule a meeting in advance.

We have technology to blame for this disturbing state of affairs. Fifty years ago, an organization's (potential) customers were *out there*, in the field. Relative to today, customers were isolated from their vendors. This was before fax machines and private branch exchange (PBX) phone systems became pervasive and certainly before email, websites, and instant messaging. Salespeople bridged this geographic divide by visiting with customers in the field—and by ferrying information back and forth between their head offices and the customers' locations.

Today, customers are no longer isolated from their vendors. Vendors' organizations are as close as the nearest web browser. Private lines, email, and instant messaging have made it easier for customers to communicate with representatives in an organization's head office than it is to communicate with their field-based salespeople.

That's right, where field salespeople historically served to reduce the friction between vendors and their customers, today it's more likely that salespeople are contributing to that friction. Certainly it's quite common to hear customers complaining that they can get better information and faster outcomes if they sidestep salespeople and communicate directly with the customer service teams based in the vendor's head office.

Salespeople have responded to this situation with a mixture of defiance and pragmatism. As suggested earlier, most have retreated inside, where they can be more productive. If they're not welcome in corporate offices, they have built their own home offices. But these same salespeople (and their managers) will vehemently defend the traditional model when challenged. Even in environments in which most transactions are repeat purchases of commodity products, salespeople will argue that sales is essentially a field activity and that customers should be prepared to pay a premium for the value that field salespeople add.

Rather than wading into that argument, let's take a moment to view sales from the customer's perspective. Ask yourself the following: If *you* are making a purchase (of an unspecified nature), is your default starting point to look for a person who can come and visit with you in the field? I suspect not!

It's more likely that your first instinct will be to turn to a medium that enables you to purchase with no human contact whatsoever, if one exists. If you need to communicate with a human in order to make your purchase, you'd probably prefer a phone conversation rather than a face-to-face visit, unless for some reason the latter is critical. And even if a face-to-face visit *is* critical, there's a good chance you'd rather visit the salesperson than have one come to your home or place of work.

Now, you might argue that I've stacked the deck in my favor by failing to specify the nature of the purchase. After all, isn't there a difference between purchasing a set of replacement razor blades and purchasing a custom-engineered software application? Let's explore that.

In the case of the replacement razor blades, it's clear that there's no value in human contact. I think most people would rather make the purchase in a single click on Amazon.

But, in the case of the custom-engineered software application, isn't it clear that you'd need to interact with a salesperson, face to face? Sure. But it's pretty unlikely that this is where your purchasing process would *start*. It's more likely that you'll start with online research. Then, at your leisure, you'll have one or more conversations with telephone advisors. Although it's clear that, at some point, you'll schedule one or more face-to-face meetings, it's likely that you will defer these meetings until you absolutely need them—perhaps simply as a hands-on workshop.

It's easy to see how the JSG sales model described in the first two chapters of this book is appropriate in engineer-to-order environments (e.g., custom-engineered software). However, it's important to recognize that transactions of this nature are a small percentage of total transactions for most organizations. Even in the case of an organization that sells only custom software, there are likely to be transactions that are simple in nature (e.g., the addition of small features to existing applications), and don't require in-person interactions.

It's time now to envision the kind of sales function that will support your (and most likely, your customers') preferred approach to purchasing.

THE INSIDE-OUT APPROACH

This fundamental change in market dynamics requires that we make an ideological shift. The salesperson's pragmatism won't cut it. We need to embrace this change and recognize that, today, sales is essentially an inside activity.

Where planning is concerned, what's required is an *inside-out* approach. Start with an inside sales function and then add field resources as they are required—and only to the extent that they are required.

Customer Service

The inside-out approach starts with attention to the type of transactions that make up the lion's share of a typical organization's revenue. These are simple—and typically repetitive—transactions. For the purpose of this book, I'm not treating these transactions as *sales*, but they're critical nonetheless.

Customer service should handle these simple transactions, and should generate quotations and handle customer issues. (A percentage of these transactions should actually bypass customer service and go direct to ecommerce, but that's outside the scope of this book.)

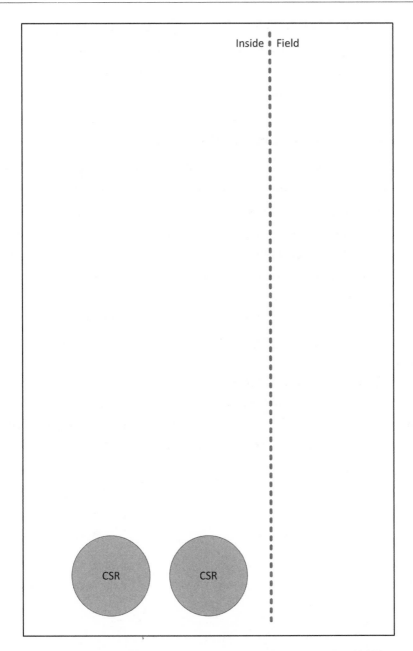

Figure 14. The inside-out approach: Customer service representatives (CSR).

Customer service should triage all inbound telephone traffic and intercept all simple orders, requests for quotes, and issues (technical questions,

delivery problems, and the like). Customer service should have sufficient protective capacity to enable the team to handle peak loads and to ensure that no one else in the organization need ever process an order, generate a quote, or handle a customer issue.

Inside Sales and Campaign Coordination

Once customer service has control over simple transactions, most executives assume that the next team to add is field sales. There are two problems with jumping straight to field sales.

First, field sales is incredibly expensive relative to inside sales. An inside salesperson can comfortably have thirty meaningful selling interactions (including email) a day, whereas a field salesperson will work hard to average four meetings.

Second, if you start with field sales, you will turn your back on a number of potential selling interactions when you insist that each prospect accept a field visit.

And this is a critical point! It's easy for sales managers to argue (as they do) that field meetings are more effective than phone conversations. However, this argument ignores the fact that an insistence on field meetings results in salespeople having fewer selling conversations overall.

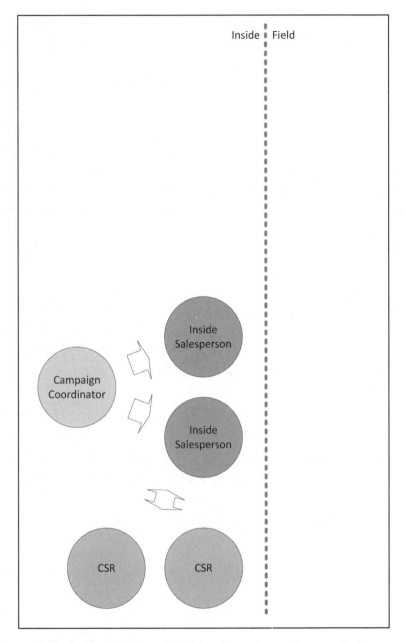

Figure 15. The inside-out approach: Inside sales and campaign coordinator.

Our inside sales team actually consists of two roles.

We have the inside salespeople, who perform nothing other than what we call *meaningful selling interactions*. These interactions include phone conversations, email communication, and even instant messaging. Of course, inside salespeople do not generate quotes or enter orders; these tasks are routed to customer service.

We also have a campaign coordinator, who is responsible for generating all of the *outbound* sales opportunities that keep the inside sales team members so busy. The campaign coordinator ensures that inside salespeople always have calls to perform and avoids inside salespeople's searching for sales opportunities within the customer relationship management application (CRM).

Field Specialists

Once you have an inside sales team, you should continue to resist the temptation to add field salespeople for just a little while longer. When you consider the incredible productivity differential, you should make sure that you've fully exploited the potential of inside sales before you add (traditional) salespeople.

So let me unpack that somewhat-opaque advice for you. By *exploit the potential of inside sales*, I mean that you should keep adding inside sales-people until the contribution margin you expect your next salesperson to generate approaches their total cost. With the phrase *traditional salespeople*, I'm hinting that it might be possible to use a special breed of salesperson to further exploit the capability of inside sales.

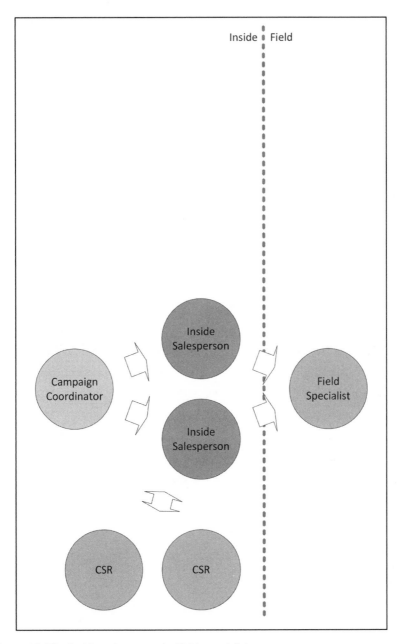

Figure 16. The inside-out approach: Field specialist.

A *field specialist* is a person who supports inside sales by performing discrete field activities. These activities are likely to be technical or semitechnical in nature. Their typical activities would include on-site requirement discovery and product demonstrations. The field specialist can also perform field visits that are requested of them by the customer service team.

Unlike a salesperson in an engineer-to-order environment (think Jennifer at JSG), field specialists are not primarily responsible for critical selling conversations; those are the responsibility of the inside sales team. Rather, the field specialist is responsible for performing field activities that would otherwise block the inside sales team from selling.

Business Development

Once you have fully exploited the potential of inside sales, both by growing the team and by supporting inside salespeople with field specialists, it's *now* time to consider traditional field salespeople. And, as you learned in the previous chapter, field salespeople (business-development managers) are tenfold more productive when we partner them with dedicated coordinators and project leaders.

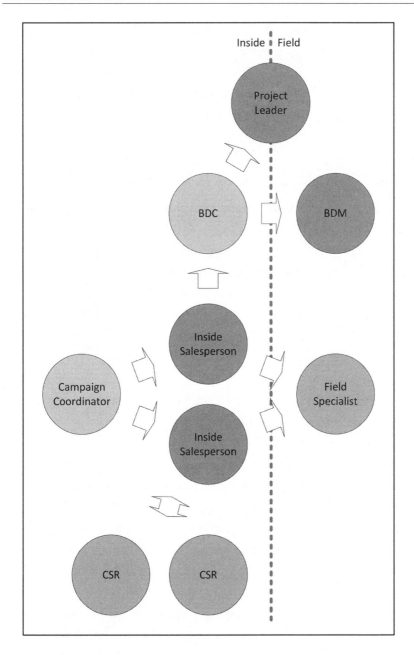

Figure 17. The inside-out approach: Business development.

We now have an outline of the entire inside-out sales function, at least at a conceptual level. We also have an understanding about how, in practice, it makes sense to go about building your sales function.

In short, start with customer service and add additional components only when you are sure you have fully exploited the existing ones.

WHAT IS THE POTENTIAL OF INSIDE SALES?

Many executives are uncomfortable with this approach, because it's based on the assumption that inside salespeople are capable of making many of the sales that are currently being made by field salespeople today. In my experience, this assumption is absolutely valid.

There are situations in which face-to-face selling conversations are absolutely critical. But there are many more situations in which they are simply not. And, as we discussed earlier, an overestimation of the requirement for face-to-face meetings tends to result in a much lower overall volume of selling conversations.

It's helpful to consider the two situations in which face-to-face meetings are genuinely required. They are critical when an activity that needs to be performed cannot be done effectively from a remote location. An obvious example would be a meeting between an architect and a landowner to discuss ideas about how to exploit the features of a piece of land. Another example would be a full-day strategic-planning workshop.

A face-to-face meeting can also be very beneficial when a potential customer is contemplating a purchasing decision that involves high levels of uncertainty. For example, if you are not a lawyer and you are considering appointing a lawyer to represent you in a particularly important case, you would feel compelled to meet your proposed counsel face to face. As a nonlawyer, you lack the ability to make an objective assessment of the individual's professional capabilities, and you have little choice (for better or worse) but to use your assessment of the person as a proxy for their professional capabilities. Conversations that do not fall into one of these categories are better performed by telephone (or email) and, increasingly, this is what potential customers prefer.

Furthermore, if you think about it, each of the face-to-face conversations described in the two categories above will undoubtedly have been preceded by quite a number of non-face-to-face conversations. In the inside-out model described in this chapter, those preliminary conversations would have been performed either by an inside salesperson or by a business-development coordinator (or both), depending on the environment.

In summary, then, it's likely that a good percentage of your sales opportunities do not require field visits at all. Furthermore, of the total field visits required, it's likely that a good number of them do not involve true selling conversations (these are the visits that consist of on-site requirements discovery or product demonstrations).

Where the staffing of your sales function is concerned, this has two implications. The first is that you need very few field representatives; and of the field representatives you do need, most will be field specialists. This in turn means it will be easier to justify spending the bigger dollars you will inevitably need to spend in order to attract the small number of capable, enterprise-class salespeople needed in your few remaining business-development manager positions. The other implication, of course, is that you need a larger inside sales team. The good news is that this enables you to exploit some economies of scale. A lively, fun inside sales environment will be a lot more appealing to a broader range of candidates then a Rolodex and a rental car. In addition, a larger team of (colocated) individuals will be much easier to manage and, consequently, may even enable you to justify the addition of a high-powered inside sales supervisor (which can have an enormous impact on team performance).

WHO ARE THESE INSIDE SALESPEOPLE?

Let me start by stressing who these inside salespeople are NOT. Your inside sales team members are not telemarketers (in the traditional sense of the word). They are true salespeople—equivalent in every sense to the type of person you would otherwise have in the field. They are knowledgeable, ambitious, and engaging. And they are paid roughly what they would expect to earn if they were field salespeople.

And, importantly, your inside sales team members are not second-class salespeople relative to your field specialists. Your inside sales team, if your organization is typical, is your primary sales team, and it's vital that this is reflected in your cultural norms.

As was hinted above, this shift in focus to inside salespeople will give you more degrees of freedom when it comes to attracting talent. You can attract capable people (perhaps from a technical background) who would simply not be interested in operating in the field. What's more, because you have team members operating in close proximity to one another, it's easier for you to introduce less-experienced candidates—meaning that you can employ younger team members or recruit people from outside your specific industry.

❊ ❊ ❊ ❊

This chapter completes your understanding of what we call the *inside-out model*. This model is a blend of customer service, inside sales (supported by the campaign coordinator and field specialists), and business development (supported by project leaders).

In chapter 6, we'll talk about alternative models and gain insight into how to apply the four key principles to design applications of sales process engineering for different environments. But first, it's time to reflect on the integration between sales and the rest of the organization.

Chapter 5
THE MACHINE WITHIN THE MACHINE

In most discussions of sales, the greater organization doesn't rate a mention. This is more than an idle curiosity. The fact that we traditionally consider the sales function in isolation is likely to be an admission of a fundamental flaw in the design of sales—as well as the cause of many of the problems we experience.

This chapter presents a model for the organization as a whole and exposes the critical connections between sales and the other key organizational functions. We'll start with the goal of the organization and drill down to discover what the sales function must do—not to be successful in isolation but to contribute to the success of the entire organization.

THE THEORY OF CONSTRAINTS: A CRASH COURSE

Although this book contains many implicit references to the theory of constraints (TOC), this chapter formally introduces some of TOC's key concepts. TOC is a process-engineering methodology, developed by Eliyahu Goldratt and popularized in his 1984 best seller *The Goal*. In short, TOC recognizes that the output of any system is determined by the system's lowest-capacity resource and that this resource (the constraint) can be used to gather intelligence about—and exercise control over—the system as a whole.

In practice, TOC enables an alternative approach to management decision making. The difference between these approaches is best highlighted with a familiar scenario:

Imagine that we are manning the ticket counter for a discount airline. A backpacker approaches and offers to buy a ticket for a domestic flight at half the standard price. The posted price for tickets is $200, so the backpacker offers to pay $100. We have received advice from our head-office finance department that tickets must be sold at $150 in order for the airline to achieve profitability. The question then is should we accept the backpacker's proposition?

Our finance department's calculus informs us that tickets should, on average, be sold for $150. That would suggest that the backpacker should be sent packing. However, the alternative is to assume that the airline will be more profitable if it banks this $100 than it will be if it holds out for $150 and ends up banking $0.

There are problems with both the first approach (fully loaded costing) and the second (marginal costing). The fully loaded approach assumes that the sale of one more ticket will trigger cost increases that propagate throughout the entire organization. The marginal approach assumes that selling one more ticket has no impact on costs (other than the cost of a bag of peanuts, that is).

The TOC approach is to recognize that well-managed systems have, at any point in time, just one constraint. This means that the system-wide implications of any decision are limited to the implications of that decision at *the constraint*, assuming the decision doesn't cause the constraint to move.

To return to our ticket counter, the TOC approach would enable us to recognize that it makes sense to accept $100 for a ticket if—and only if—(a) our backpacker does not displace a passenger who is prepared to pay more and (b) selling this additional ticket does not cause us to incur excessive additional costs (such as scheduling a new flight).

The solution, then, is to sell the backpacker a standby ticket that can only be redeemed on an undersold flight (and only minutes before takeoff).

Now, this scenario is familiar because we all fly on planes, but we don't necessarily apply this decision-making approach to our own businesses. My point is that we probably should!

THE GOAL

Let's start our consideration of the greater organization at the beginning—with the goal. Considering that, in this book, I contemplate just one type of organization (a business), the goal is obvious: to make money. And, at a glance, the contribution that sales must make to the achievement of this goal also appears obvious: to make sales.

But, not so fast! Does it automatically follow that, if the sales function generates more sales, the organization makes more money?

Actually, it doesn't. There are two common cases in which the sales function can actually harm the greater organization by generating more sales. Sales can sell something that production doesn't have the ability or capacity to produce to the customer's requirements (damaging goodwill as a consequence), or sales can sell something that causes the organization to make less money than it otherwise would (e.g., a transaction that causes limited production resources to be diverted from activities that would generate greater value).

We must recognize, then, that the objective of sales cannot be defined in isolation. It must reference at least one other organizational function. (And the same can be said for each of the other functions.) We should also suspect that, because organizations can differ significantly from one another, it may not be possible to specify the objective with a standard statement that is applicable in every circumstance.

THE CONSTRAINT

As I've mentioned, a business consists of a number of functions that must work together to make money (the goal). How much money the business makes is determined, to a large extent, by how well these functions work together.

Let's consider a very simple business, consisting of just *sales* and *production* functions.

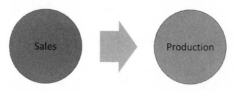

Figure 18. Model of a simple business.

In order to make money, the business must generate a gross profit (or, technically, a contribution margin) at a faster rate than it incurs operating expenses. Units of gross profit must be processed by both sales and production before they can be banked. Specifically, sales must win an order, and then production must fulfill it.

We will use the term *throughput* to refer to units of gross profit. Technically, throughput is equal to the revenue generated by a transaction minus the totally variable costs associated with that transaction (e.g., raw material costs, sales commissions, shipping).

Because the amount of money that a business makes is a function of the *rate* at which it processes throughput, it is important that we understand the capacity of the business. In other words, we need to know how much throughput the business can process in a given period.

The capacity of the business as a whole is determined by the capacity of its lowest-capacity function—what we'll call *the constraint*.

Figure 19. Sales is the constraint.

So, if the capacity of each of the functions in our simple business is that in figure 19, this business can generate only $T10,000 a day ($T is *throughput dollars*). Production has the capacity to produce more, but without sales to fulfill, there's no point in attempting to do so.

Because (in this scenario) sales determines the profitability of the organization as a whole, we can draw some conclusions about how sales and production should work together. Sales should sell as much as possible (in this scenario, it *does* make sense for sales to sell as much as possible). Production should produce whatever has been sold by the sales team, and nothing more.

We can now generalize from these conclusions and arrive at two simple rules applicable to *every* business:

1. The constraint should operate at full capacity, at all times.
2. Nonconstraints should subordinate to the constraint.

In this context, in which sales is the constraint, sales should always operate at full capacity (i.e., it should sell as much as possible), and production should *subordinate* to sales, meaning that production should match the ordered volume.

If we reverse the capacities of the functions in our simple business, as in figure 20, in which sales outperforms production capacity, production becomes the constraint, and sales should subordinate to it.

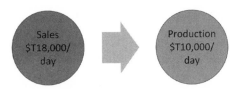

Figure 20. Production is the constraint.

This scenario leads to the conclusion that sales should sell only what production has the capacity to produce, and production should operate at full capacity at all times.

Variability

We must acknowledge that, in reality, the output of any resource is inherently variable. When we talk about a person, a machine, or a plant producing an output of *x*, what we really mean is that the output *averages* that value. If we plot the output of any resource on a run-chart, we will likely discover that the output is quite variable, such as in figure 21.

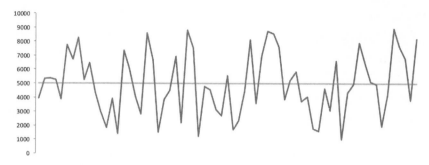

Figure 21. This inside salesperson might average $5,000 in sales a day, but the range is greater than the mean.

This means that, continuing with our example, it is impractical for sales to aim to provide production with $T10,000 worth of orders a day, for two reasons: The output of sales will vary dramatically from day to day (that is the nature of sales), and the capacity of production will also vary; but it's variability will be independent of—and therefore out of sync with—that of sales. If sales were to attempt to provide production with $T10,000 worth of orders a day, production would find that it is regularly starved of work—meaning that the actual output of the organization would be *less* than the capacity of production. ($T = throughput or contribution margin.)

The solution to this problem requires that sales maintain a buffer of orders upstream from production, large enough to absorb the sales function's inherent variability—but no larger.

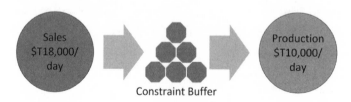

Figure 22. A buffer protects the capacity of the constraint.

The existence of the buffer enables the organization to fully exploit its production capacity, as well as to maintain good on-time delivery performance. With this small but critical modification to our simple business, we can now finalize our directives to each function: Sales should maintain the constraint buffer at its optimal size, and production should operate at full capacity at all times.

As was promised, *variability* also points us to the reason why an organization should have a single constraint. The inherent variability in the output of every resource means that an attempt to balance the capacities of resources is a fool's errand. In an environment in which all resources have identical average capacities, the day-to-day variation in actual output will result in the emergence of a constraint that wanders, unpredictably, from resource to resource—rendering the organization unmanageable.

It makes more sense for management to determine which function should be the constraint and then build enough protective capacity in nonconstraint resources to ensure that the system is stable.

THE OPTIMAL CONSTRAINT LOCATION

That's right; you get to choose the location of the constraint within your organization. (Well, you do if—and only if—you can stop the cost accountants from attempting to balance the capacities of all resources!)

To shed some light on this decision, let's meet one of our silent revolutionaries prior to their transition.

Pace Press is a traditional plate and ink printer. Its owner has stayed current with technology and has, consequently, seen Pace's production capacity increase geometrically over the last fifteen years. The owner's not-insignificant investment in technology has produced a dramatic improvement in plant efficiency, measured on a per-impression (per-printed-page) basis.

However, Pace's sales team has failed to keep up with production. The plant has the capacity to generate around $600,000 a month in throughput, but the sales team is selling less than a third of that. The owner is rapidly realizing that the efficiencies produced by the new technology are a mirage if the additional capacity is not sold.

Clearly, in Pace's case, sales is the system constraint, meaning that we can apply our two rules to define objectives for both sales and production. But advising sales to sell as much as possible—and production to keep pace—is not much of a solution when two-thirds of Pace's plant capacity is sitting unused.

It makes more sense to pause and examine the overall design of the organization. And, in so doing, the very first question we should ask is: *Which function should be the organizational constraint?*

To answer that question, we must start at the beginning: with the goal of the organization.

We know that Pace's goal is to make money, but it's worth exploring what *make money* really means. Clearly, it means more than simply generating revenues; you can generate a lot of revenue and still go broke. It must also mean more than making profits; profits are good, but they are only half of the story. In full context, *making money* means maximizing the return on the owners' equity, and you can do this by increasing the *return,* decreasing the *equity,* or some combination of the two.

This better understanding of the goal helps us to recognize that, because production is where almost all of the owner's equity is invested, production should probably be Pace's constraint, not sales.

So, in the short run, our two rules may provide Pace Press with a thumb in the leaking dike, but in the long run, Pace must dramatically increase the capacity of the sales function, to the point that sales can consistently sell *more* than production has the capacity to produce. (Theoretically, Pace could also downsize production capacity, but this is rarely an appealing option.)

Once Pace has remedied this immediate problem—and shifted the constraint to production—the responsibility of sales will no longer be to sell as much as possible. Sales will be responsible for maintaining a queue of orders upstream from production, orders large enough to ensure that production operates at full capacity, day in and day out.

Because Pace is one of our silent revolutionaries, you can probably guess that they chose to dramatically increase the capacity of sales. Today the presses at Pace run at 100-percent utilization, 100 percent of the time. Pace's salespeople are no longer looking for something—anything!—to print. Instead, they search constantly for ways to increase the yield that Pace Print earns on its finite plant capacity.

THE THIRD FUNCTION: NEW PRODUCT DEVELOPMENT

Now that we understand the concept of *the constraint*, we need a more complete model of the organization. To date, we've envisaged just two functions: sales and production.

In the long run, however, a business needs one more function in order to thrive: *new product development* (or *engineering*).

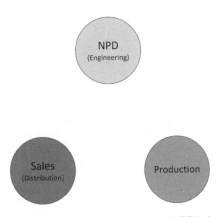

Figure 23. The addition of new product development (NPD) gives us a more complete model of the business.

The primary responsibility of new product development (NPD) is to conceptualize and design the products (or services) that sales sells and that production delivers. In addition, NPD will often innovate internally, creating better production or distribution processes.

It's critical that we explicitly recognize the existence—and the importance—of NPD. It's not just that NPD keeps the organization relevant in the long run; in most organizations, NPD will determine whether potential customers are prepared to entertain your salespeople!

Now obviously all organizations have more functions than those examined here (e.g., finance, administration), but because these are *support* functions, they have no bearing on this discussion. Similarly, I am choosing to exclude senior management from the model, because I'm assuming that senior management is creating the model in the first place!

With our model expanded to three functions, determining the ideal constraint location becomes a little trickier (see figure 24). However, if we consider the three value-chain configurations we discussed in chapter 2, the optimal constraint location starts to come into focus.

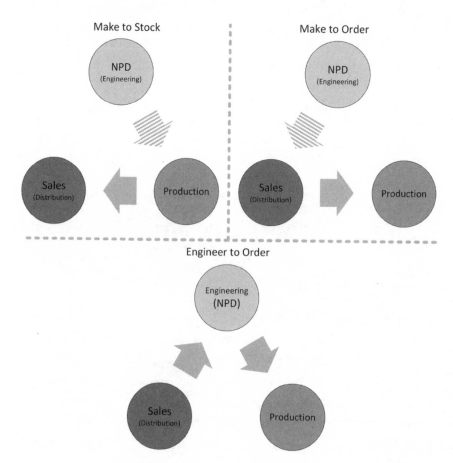

Figure 24. The three value-chain configurations.

Make to Stock

A traditional car company is an example of a make-to-stock (MTS) manufacturer. (Because services cannot be stockpiled, the term MTS applies purely to manufacturers.) The flow is simple: NPD designs something, then production manufacturers it, and sales sells it, as in the left panel of figure 24.

As for the question of which function should be the organization's constraint, this is evident from the phrase *make to stock*. As we discussed previously, the stockpile of inventory exists to buffer production from distribution—meaning that sales must be the constraint.

In most cases, the flow between NPD and sales is asynchronous (hence the striped arrow above). In other words, NPD designs new products periodically, not once for each item manufactured.

Make to Order

Production does not commence for a make-to-order (MTO) provider until the order is received. Accordingly, there can be no inventory of finished goods.

Increasingly, technology allows even traditional manufacturers (think car companies) to move to an MTO configuration. Dell is a perfect example of an MTO manufacturer—as is a tax agent or a traditional printer. An MTO provider does not have to design a new product for each customer; rather, it's a case of configuring standard options to suit the customer's specifications.

The MTO workflow looks like this: NPD designs a product (or service) with a finite number of customizable options, then sales sells the product—and helps the customer customize it to suit their requirements—and, finally, production produces it.

In most cases, the ideal constraint location for an MTO producer will be production. The responsibility of sales (as in our Pace example) should be to maintain a queue of orders upstream from production. Furthermore, this queue of orders should ideally maximize the yield on production's limited capacity, bearing in mind that different types of work will have varying impacts on the profitability of the organization.

An interesting example of an MTO provider is a funeral home. At first glance, it would appear impossible for a funeral home to maintain a queue of orders upstream from production (the mortuary). The reality, however, is that, in recent years, funeral homes have figured out how to do exactly this. Most funeral homes today have sales teams that sell funeral plans—meaning that, when a person passes, their funeral has already been arranged and paid for.

Engineer to Order

Engineer-to-order (ETO) environments add another level of complexity to MTO. Rather than configuring a product or service to suit a customer's requirements, an ETO provider *designs* a custom solution, and, in most cases, the design procedure spans the point of sale. In other words, in an ETO environment, the vendor will most likely need to do some preliminary design to win the job and will then have to complete the design *after* the job is won.

In most ETO environments, engineering should be maintained as the organizational constraint. This is because engineering is the source of the firm's competitive advantage and because engineering is, in most cases, harder to scale than sales or production (remember that components of production can generally be outsourced).

Examples of ETO providers include engineering and architecture firms, traditional- and web-design companies, and enterprise-software providers.

A New Objective for Sales

If we adjust our diagram to indicate the optimal constraint location for each value-chain configuration, we now have our final model. In each case, the constraint is the resource downstream from the constraint buffer.

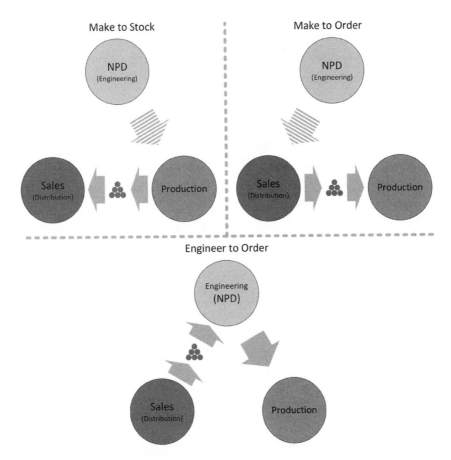

Figure 25. Constraint locations for the three value chain configurations.

In summary then, what we are proposing is that in each case, the constrained function—and only the constrained function—operate at 100-percent utilization and that the other functions *subordinate* to the constraint. For each resource, to *subordinate* means something a little different: NPD subordinates (in MTS and MTO environments) by ensuring that product or service offerings are consistently appealing to the market, meaning that they are innovative and that they can be competitively priced. Production subordinates to distribution in an MTS environment by ensuring that inventory stockpiles are the optimal size and composition. Too little inventory will mean running out of stock, and too much inventory will cause distribution to liquidate unsold items or, alternatively, will prevent the uptake of newer lines. Sales subordinates in MTO and ETO environments by ensuring that a queue of orders is maintained upstream from either production or engineering—and by ensuring that the composition of this queue maximizes the yield on the downstream function's finite capacity.

We can now see that it's only in the case of the MTS environment that the objective of sales should be to sell as much as possible. In the other two environments, sales should subordinate to either production or engineering.

And, as I mentioned earlier, over time organizations tend to transition from MTS to either MTO or ETO. This means that it is increasingly unlikely that your sales function is—or at least should be—the organizational constraint.

If you are not an MTS manufacturer and your sales manager believes that their responsibility is to maximize sales, you should suspect that this is evidence of an organizational design problem. If it does not make sense for sales to be your organizational constraint, sales should have enough protective capacity to enable it to maintain a queue of orders upstream from either production or engineering at all times.

If sales is resourced properly, your sales manager will never claim that it's their responsibility to maximize sales. It would be obvious to them that this would cause the order queue to quickly inflate to the point at which lead times would explode and customer relationships would be damaged. If you consider that the sales function exhibits a greater degree of variability than all other functions, it should be clear that you need a good deal of protective capacity in sales to enable that function to subordinate effectively.

As was mentioned, it's not just the size of the order queue that's important in MTO and ETO environments; it's the composition of that queue. Sales should be responsible for selling the mix of work that maximizes the yield on either production's or engineering's finite resources.

The Optimal Mix

Now, the notion of constraints applies at the functional—as well as the organizational—level. In other words, if your organizational constraint is your production function, the production function will be constrained (at any one point in time) by a single production resource.

In Pace's case, production is now the organizational constraint. However, if we look inside production, we discover that the plant is designed to ensure that a bank of shiny new five-color Heidelbergs operates at 100-percent capacity at all times. The other production resources subordinate to that bank of printing presses.

If Pace's sales manager wants to maximize the profitably of Pace (which I can assure you he does), he will plan promotional and sales activities with a view to (in this order) keeping those printing presses fully loaded with work, prioritizing jobs that maximize the yield on the Heidelbergs' limited capacity, and identifying opportunities to sell any spare capacity in the plant that may not put a load on the presses (e.g., it might be possible to opportunistically sell some spare capacity in the bindery department to a print broker).

It should be clear that this tight integration of sales and production will have a profound impact on the profitability of the firm—as, indeed, it has in Pace's case. And the importance of tight integration (discussed in the previous chapter) is even more critical in an ETO environment, in which the line between sales and production is blurred.

For this reason, in MTO and ETO environments, the new approach to the design of the sales function, presented in this book, offers much more than the opportunity to build a more efficient sales function. By allowing the tight integration of sales with other functions, this new model will affect almost every facet of customer engagement.

A Word of Caution

The model presented in this chapter is intended as a ready reckoner—not as a substitute for a formal approach to strategy formulation. As well as the value-chain configuration, you should also consider the source of your organization's competitive advantage. For example, because movie studios and drug companies tend to compete on the basis of continual and rapid innovation, NPD (or research and development) should always be their organizational constraint (remembering that the constraint is the only function that operates at 100-percent utilization).

And, as I suggested earlier, it's worth paying attention to how the owner's equity is distributed among the functions. If, for example, a particular function is particularly difficult or expensive to scale, it may make sense to maintain this function as the organization constraint.

And in the case of organizations that consist of a single function (e.g., print brokers and travel agencies), the identification of the optimal organizational constraint should be relatively easy!

❄ ❄ ❄ ❄

More often than not, breakthrough results require more than just a redesign of the sales function. True breakthroughs often come from a better integration of sales with one or more other functions. In other words, this means a redesign of the entire organization, not just sales.

If this chapter has you thinking, you might want to add *The Goal* to your reading list.

Chapter 6
ONE BIG IDEA, MANY POSSIBLE APPLICATIONS

Executives who encounter sales process engineering (SPE) for the first time will often ask whether it's applicable in all situations. The answer to this question—not surprisingly—is *no*. Few theories—if any—can legitimately claim to be valid in all contexts.

However, we should be careful answering this question. The questioner often wants to know whether a *specific application of SPE* is applicable in all environments. That's quite a different question! This person may have read only chapter 1 of this book, or they may have observed an application of SPE in a colleague's business. Either way, it's dangerous to confuse SPE with particular applications of the larger theory.

SPE, as we've discussed, consists of a central idea (the division of labor) and four key principles. It's possible to derive quite a number of applications of SPE from the theory itself. These applications allow SPE to be applied to a remarkable range of sales environments—but not *all* sales environments.

This chapter will identify the limitations of SPE and will introduce you to a number of applications of the theory. And, I hope, it will provide some insight into how to create your own application of SPE to suit your particular sales function.

When SPE Doesn't Make Sense

Because the essence of SPE is the division of labor, SPE doesn't make sense in those environments in which the division of labor doesn't make sense. This may be the case either because the organization will not benefit from increasing the productivity of the sales function or because the efficiency gains from specialization are offset by a significant escalation of costs. Consider these three fictitious scenarios.

1. Alpha Corp's new-product-development team has scored a home run with its latest device: a data projector. The projector's combination of small size, low cost, and super-high-intensity beam has resulted in the device becoming a must-have item for executives and salespeople. Since this new projector hit the market, orders have eclipsed Alpha's manufacturing capacity—meaning that crowd control has, for the indefinite future, become the sole responsibility of the Alpha sales team.

2. When Beta International inked its deal with the US military, it committed to providing representatives in eight European countries. These representatives' primary responsibility is customer service; and for this reason, Beta was careful to employ locals (who speak the local languages). In each country, there is a small number of additional sales opportunities that Beta is keen to exploit; however, the potential is not significant enough to justify the addition of business-development coordinators (BDCs)—let alone specialist salespeople, especially when you consider that multiple individuals would be required in order to cover the range of languages spoken on this continent.

3. Charlie Inc. has a neat product but no sales function. The product is Internet security—delivered as a web service rather than as an application. The problem is that Charlie Inc. has no idea how it should distribute this product. Should it sell direct to small businesses, or through resellers (electronics retailers and telcos, perhaps)? Charlie Inc. is not even sure whether the small-business or the residential market is likely to be more responsive. At this point, Charlie Inc. is less interested in efficiency than in agility. It makes no sense to build sales infrastructure until it has a distribution strategy.

It's clear that in these scenarios there is no case for the division of labor—and, therefore, none for SPE. But it should also be fairly obvious that each of these situations is more the exception than the rule.

It's time, then, to consider more-common situations—those in which the case for the division of labor is strong.

THE INSIDE-OUT MODEL

We concluded chapter 4 with what we call the *inside-out model,* which is a blend of two applications. This is the model most frequently implemented in mid- to large-sized organizations. The power of this model is that it supports the large range of transaction (and opportunity) types that you typically encounter in a larger organization.

It's easy to understand the power of this model when you consider a typical scenario:

ERM builds mining machines to order. Primarily, ERM is a make-to-order manufacturer, but, like many larger organizations, it also custom-engineers machines for major projects and sells a range of smaller machines (and parts) from stock. As a consequence, ERM processes an enormous diversity of transactions (and opportunities) that range from an inbound order for a replacement part all the way to a three-year quest to conceptualize and sell a custom three-million-dollar machine.

To add to the complexity, there are enormous imbalances between the profit contributed by and the effort expended to win and service each of these transaction and opportunity types. For this reason, it makes little sense for ERM to manage these radically different selling and transactional situations with the one SPE application—or, for that matter, with the one team of salespeople. Radically different selling situations require materially different applications of SPE.

The power of the inside-out model (figure 26) is that it can accommodate the requirements of remarkably complex environments, such as those of our mining-machine manufacturer. It can do this because it's the blend of two SPE applications.

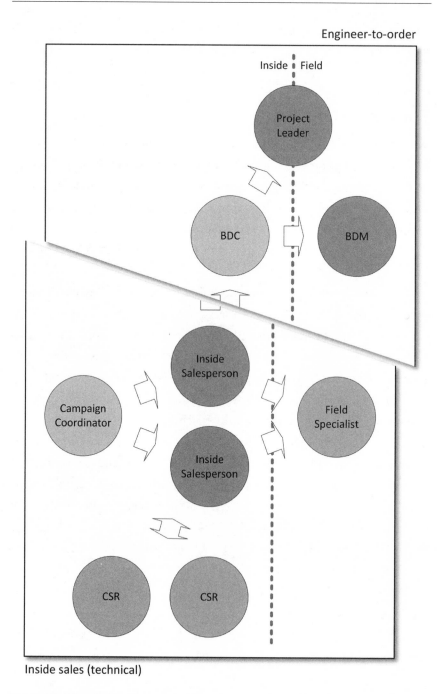

Engineer-to-order

Inside ⋮ Field

Project Leader

BDC

BDM

Inside Salesperson

Campaign Coordinator

Field Specialist

Inside Salesperson

CSR

CSR

Inside sales (technical)

Figure 26. The standard model is a blend of two SPE applications.

Inside Sales

The inside sales application is the starting point for most organizations. This is because most organizations process at least some simple and repetitive transactions.

As you know, the customer service team is responsible for inbound transactions, in addition to providing quotes and resolving issues. And outbound sales opportunities are generated by the campaign coordinator and prosecuted by inside salespeople, with the assistance of field specialists in technical sales environments.

This application can accommodate a remarkable range of transactions.

Obviously, at the low end, it's economical for inside salespeople to pursue—and for customer service representatives to process—small-dollar-value transactions. Over time, the lower-dollar-value inbound transactions should be moved to ecommerce, which you can treat as an extension of the customer service team.

More surprisingly, at the high end, I regularly see inside sales teams pursuing opportunities in the tens or even low hundreds of thousands of dollars—particularly when they are supported by technical field specialists. It's important to remember that large-dollar-value transactions can often be simple from the customer's perspective—particularly when the customer is making repeat purchases or buying replacement parts or other consumables.

Engineer-to-Order Sales

The other component of our inside-out model is the engineer-to-order application. This application makes sense when opportunities are on the other side of the complexity threshold and when most critical selling conversations genuinely do need to be performed in the field. As well as classic engineer-to-order environments, this application makes sense for higher-dollar-value enterprise and government sales.

In this model, we pair a field-based business-development manager (BDM) with an office-based business-development coordinator (BDC).

In addition, we support the BDM with a field-based technical expert (the project leader).

In most cases, this application is paired with the inside sales application (per the inside-out model), but in cases in which it is not, a campaign coordinator would also be required. As I've mentioned, in the inside-out model, sales opportunities are typically generated for the BDC by the inside sales team.

SPECIAL CASES

The inside-out model is flexible enough to suit most organizations (including ERM, the mining equipment manufacturer). But, of course, there are special cases. Following are three, with an application that makes sense for each.

Indirect Sales

Specialist Workwear is a Canadian manufacturer and importer of specialty work clothing. Many years ago, Specialist's salespeople sold direct to end users—their customers are manufacturers, distributors, mining companies, and similar organizations. Recently, however, it has made sense for their customers to rationalize their procurement—buying clothing, along with other safety products—from intermediaries.

Specialist had to choose between continuing to focus on work-wear—and distributing through intermediaries—or broadening their focus to become direct vendors of general safety products. They chose the former—and continue to embrace this direction by maintaining a healthy pipeline of innovative new products.

Predictably, the switch to indirect distribution resulted in a dramatic increase in volume, along with a reduction in margin, but the change also created a complex environment for Specialist's sales team. Specialist's salespeople were used to selling direct—and derived greater satisfaction from direct sales because of the higher margins those sales generated. However, they understood the importance of maintaining sound relationships with resellers, who were responsible for large sales volumes and who were, understandably, a little touchy about direct sales. Specialist Workwear recognized that a change was required when sales plateaued and when numerous attempts to scale their existing model failed.

If you sell via intermediaries (resellers, manufacturers' representatives, agents, or distributors), it's important to recognize that the inside-out model is not appropriate for your situation.

The inside-out model involves the conversion of salespeople from autonomous agents into team members. By definition, intermediaries are not part of your team (in the strict sense of the word) and are unlikely to relish the thought of having activities pushed to them from your head office. If you distribute through intermediaries, you have two considerations: You must first confirm that this actually makes sense, as opposed to selling direct. And then, if you do confirm this, you must identify a way to improve sales without challenging your intermediaries' autonomy.

Should You Sell Directly?

As perhaps you've suspected, the inside-out model tends to weaken the argument for intermediaries. The inside-out model enables you to centralize most sales activity and to reduce your regional presence to field specialists, who don't need sales offices. This makes it easy and inexpensive for you to distribute into regions in which it wouldn't be economical with the traditional sales function.

However, as Specialist's case suggests, there are situations in which it still makes good sense to distribute via intermediaries. The two most common reasons are that existing intermediaries already possess relationships with potential customers that will be very costly to replicate, and that intermediaries represent a range of complementary products, which means either that it is more economical for the customer to deal with the intermediary than it is to deal with you directly or that the intermediary can justify an operational presence in their particular region that could not be justified with your smaller offering.

If you are going to distribute via intermediaries, it's important that you understand exactly why—and that you hold your partner accountable for the value you are expecting them to add. To remain relevant, your partner needs to outperform the sales function that you believe you could build, should you choose to do so. And, unfortunately for your partner, your reading this book is likely to result in them being held to an even higher standard!

A Positive Working Relationship—All or Nothing

Because the word *intermediary* is a little cumbersome, let's substitute the word *reseller* for the balance of this discussion, bearing in mind that a reseller might be a sales rep, a distributor, a retailer, an agent, or any similar representative.

If you are going to distribute via resellers—and if you have taken the time to confirm that this genuinely makes sense—you should make an all-or-nothing commitment to your channel. Specifically, you should promise your resellers that they will receive their full commission on all transactions that are processed by your customer service team (from their accounts, of course), and that all new-account inquiries in their territory will be routed to them.

It should go without saying that, except in isolated cases,[8] it is impossible to develop the close working relationships you need with your resellers if you are simultaneously competing with them for accounts and transactions.

But that's not the primary reason that an all-or-nothing commitment is required. The primary reason is that your organization needs to be engineered quite differently, depending on whether you are selling directly or indirectly. To attempt to do both will almost certainly result in failure to do either particularly well.

The decision to put all the wood behind the channel-management arrow was not an easy one for Specialist Workwear; it was difficult to resist the siren song of direct transactions. But the commitment had to be made. The primary concern was not the impact that these transactions would have on distributors; rather, it was the impact that it would have on Specialist *internally*. Their new strategy was a delicate thing. Any signal that it was not being executed consistently would have relegated it to the graveyard of clever ideas.

Channel Management

Once you decide to distribute via channel partners, your first task is to change your internal terminology to reflect this. From this point forward, you no longer have a sales function; you have a channel-management function. You no longer have salespeople; you have channel managers. And so on.

It's important that everyone in your organization understand that sales are being made by your resellers, and that your job is to *facilitate* those transactions—not to drive them directly. This understanding has to be reflected in your reporting. Your long-range metrics must be sales related, of course, but in the short range, you need to measure antecedents to those transactions (whatever they might be).

This brings us to the design of your channel-management application. And, of course, our discussion has to start with the division of labor.

If your channel partners are retailers, it's likely that you and they have a clear and sensible division of responsibilities. This is not the case, however, if your partners are distributers, manufacturer's reps, or resellers of a different stripe. This is because other types of resellers have evolved from traditional field salespeople. And, perhaps because of this pedigree, many have been particularly resistant to the environmental changes that are driving our conversion to an *inside-out* approach to sales.

The onus is on you, then, to determine an optimal division of responsibilities—and after reading this far, you are well prepared to do that. However, we must acknowledge that changes cannot simply be thrust on existing channel partners. It may take years to transition some partners to the model you envisage.

If you weigh your strengths against those of your resellers, you're likely to arrive at a division of responsibilities that looks something like this.

Table 2. The division of responsibilities between your organization and the reseller.

Reseller's responsibility	Your responsibility
The origination of sales opportunities within existing customer base and networks	The origination of opportunities outside of reseller's existing networks—and opportunities for new products
The management of late-stage sales opportunities	The generation of promotional materials and provision of sales technologies
Field-based service and technical support	Phone-based customer service and estimating

A division of responsibilities like that shown in table 2 will result in your resellers playing to their strengths (and you to yours). You'd like them to spend as much time in the field working with customers and as little time as possible in the office.

Take phone-based customer service, for example. If you have multiple resellers, it makes no sense for each of them to maintain their own customer service team. Why wouldn't you build a central team—even if it means having your operators answer calls using your resellers' business names?

By pooling demand, you can provide a higher level of customer care at a much lower cost. The same applies to promotions, sales technologies (e.g., the customer relationship management application [CRM], ecommerce), and some technical tasks (e.g., estimating). Assuming additional responsibilities like these increases your costs, of course, but it also enables you to create a much closer working relationship with your resellers. The trick is to use that close working relationship to exploit your new supply-chain efficiencies and drive up sales volumes.

In most cases, our silent revolutionaries build SPE applications following the channel-management application in figure 27.

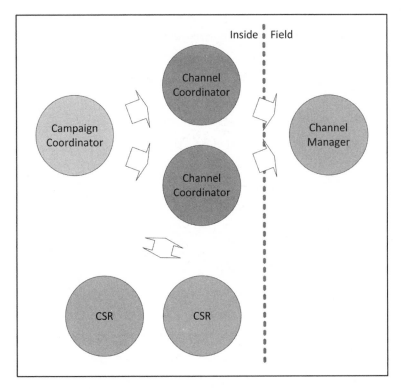

Figure 27. The channel-management application.

The field-based channel manager spends 100 percent of their time in the field (of course), and all of that time is spent with resellers and their reps—either in their facilities (e.g., training, assisting with sales, running events) or making joint calls on their customers.

The office-based channel coordinators are responsible for scheduling all of that field activity and for providing proactive assistance to the resellers and their teams. Ideally, the channel coordinators will have an open dialogue with the resellers over the status of all open opportunities.

In this application, we still have a promotions function, but it is intended to *supplement* the reseller's organic opportunity flow. The campaign coordinator administers promotional activities and pushes opportunities to the channel coordinators, who then provide them to the resellers—either directly or via channel managers.

These campaigns serve two purposes: First, they enable you to lead resellers into market segments they might not enter of their own volition. Likewise, they help you to break new products that resellers might be otherwise slow to embrace. Second, because resellers are always keen for opportunities, your promotional activities—and the opportunities they generate—provide your channel coordinators and managers with a catalyst to accelerate the development of close working relationships.

It's important to note that the sales opportunities you generate for resellers should normally be viewed as a supplement to their own opportunities. If you find yourself generating the lion's share of a reseller's opportunities, you'll probably have to conclude that the reseller relationship is past its use-by date!

When Specialist Workwear started to schedule field trips, these were a foreign concept for both channel managers and distributors. The channel managers suspected that the distributors would be unwilling to commit their time to field trips—let alone to the phone work required to line up several days' worth of customer meetings. And many distributors were a little uncomfortable with the proposition—even though its merits were obvious.

The proof, as they say, is in the tasting. The first round of field trips was sufficient to turn both the channel managers and their distributors into believers. The channel managers felt empowered by the pure focus on business development, and the distributors acknowledged that this initiative was set to multiply their volume of true sales activity—and grow their businesses as a consequence.

Another benefit of these field trips is that they require a flurry of activity between the resellers and Specialist's channel coordinators. This activity has resulted in relationships that endure, even though field trips are infrequent.

This new approach has enabled Specialist Workwear to vastly increase their geographical coverage—without increasing payroll costs. In newer territories, field trips caused an immediate and significant increase in sales volumes, and the centralization of customer service has reduced errors and issue-resolution time.

Small Business

It would be tempting to assume that SPE is not relevant to a small business because the division of labor requires an increase in its headcount. Actually, the opposite seems to be the case. A sensible application of the division of labor is helping many smaller businesses find capacity within their existing teams—even when those teams are extremely small.

Influx is an online marketing firm. In exchange for a monthly retainer, it manages its customers' online activities (e.g., websites, pay-per-click advertising, search-engine optimization, lead management).

Influx had just dismissed its third salesperson in as many years. The story, in each case, had been the same. Matthew, the founder and CEO, had recognized that competing priorities made it impossible for him to continue to drive the growth of the firm single-handedly. After combing through resumes, Matthew chose the best (or least-bad) candidate and permitted himself to be inspired by that candidate's enthusiasm—and their promise of new accounts.

In each case, the new recruit would busy themselves with critical sales preparations: creating a new set of sales aids, online market research, list building and direct mail campaigns, and so on. Days would turn into months, field visits would be occasional, and the only new accounts to come on board would be the ones that Matthew stumbled across when he wasn't busy solving production problems.

Upon contemplation, Matthew recognized that *circus master* was his unofficial job description. As Influx had grown, it had become increasingly chaotic. After three years of false starts at the development of a sales function, Matthew was open to new ideas.

The trick, where small businesses are concerned, is to focus your engineering efforts on the organization as a whole—rather than just the sales function. If a small business doesn't have a clear demarcation between sales and production, there's no point building plans that presuppose one.

The lack of consistent sales activity at Influx had led to a boom-and-bust demand cycle. When production was quiet, Matthew would find a way to drag in some work. But then as soon as production became busy again, sales activity would stop (ignoring, of course, salespeople's online research activities). This boom-and-bust cycle ensured that Influx was always under-resourced during busy times. Matthew could only afford to resource for an average load, not for peak loads.

Periodic production overloads had led to some suboptimal production behaviors. There was a production schedule, but no one paid any attention to it. Instead, each team member attempted to work simultaneously on a long list of tasks, re-sorting the list multiple times a day according to who screamed the loudest.

And, on many occasions, it was Matthew doing the screaming!

If you reflect on our discussion of the inside-out model in chapter 3, we acknowledged that, as we push toward the division of labor, the very first specialist *must* be the scheduler. The same rule applies here, but, in very small organizations, we must ensure that we apply the rule to the organization as a whole—not just to sales. When Matthew recruited Influx's first salesperson, he had attempted to leapfrog this critical step.

When Matthew's epiphany came, it came in two parts. He realized that he needed a constant volume of sales activity to eliminate the boom-and-bust problem. And he realized that discipline was needed in both production and sales: The schedule had to be sacrosanct, multitasking had to be eliminated, and commitments could be made only if they could be honored without all-night vigils.

Matthew's first step was to resign his circus master responsibilities and employ a dedicated *master scheduler*. In exchange, Matthew agreed to volunteer just 30 percent of his capacity to be used for business-development meetings. In recognition of the fact that his business didn't have—and couldn't afford—discrete sales and production functions, Matthew resolved to maintain one schedule for the business as a whole.

Influx's new master scheduler (a smart young graduate) was responsible for planning both sales and production activities onto an enormous whiteboard, occupying pride-of-place in Influx's foyer. From day one, the master scheduler was schooled in one critical condition: Regardless of production demands, Matthew *must* be scheduled to perform ten meaningful selling conversations a week. And if the opportunities from which to schedule those activities did not already exist, the scheduler *must* schedule the necessary activities required to manifest those opportunities.

In addition, every person (including Matthew) at Influx was schooled in one other critical condition: *The schedule was final.* Each person performed *only* the tasks assigned to them and *only* in the assigned sequence, and *only* the scheduler had the authority to change the schedule.

Influx's situation is all too common for small businesses. This chaotic situation is the rule, not the exception; and this counterproductive environment cannibalizes resources that could otherwise be used to sell more and to deliver orders on time.

When money is tight, it can be tough to concede that what's required is not a sales or production person but a *scheduler*—a person who neither sells nor produces. But, in situations like these, a master scheduler truly is the critical requirement. It enables a small business to solve its two most pressing problems by ensuring a *consistent* volume of sales activity, which in time will lead to a steady order flow, and by applying discipline to production scheduling, which will eliminate chaos and effectively increase the organization's production capacity. This is shown in figure 28.

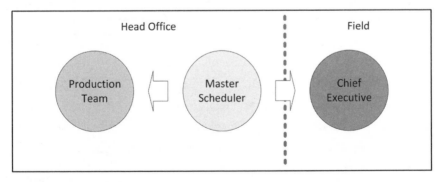

Figure 28. The small-business application.

An obvious benefit of this model is that it results in the chief executive—rather than a salesperson—doing the selling. Aside from saving money, this is a good idea because the chief executive is likely to be a better salesperson than an employee, and because it will be relatively easy for the master scheduler to book appointments for the chief executive. Once this model is in place, it is quite easy to transition to the inside-out model in increments as the organization grows.

Matthew cannot foresee Influx adding a dedicated salesperson anytime in the foreseeable future. The changes he made had little immediate effect. After a little grumbling, the production team members got used to working on discrete tasks as the tasks were allocated to them. Matthew certainly appreciated the ten sales calls that appeared in his calendar each week—although he did notice that the increase in volume was somewhat offset by a reduction in quality.

The benefits of these changes became apparent in two waves. First, the team noticed that the chaos had disappeared. The team members began to work normal hours, and conflict was eliminated, along with rework—previously, the bane of everyone's existence. With on-time delivery performance improving, Matthew found himself in a position to make more aggressive promises to potential clients, and to make them with greater conviction.

Matthew didn't really appreciate the increase in sales (the second wave) until, one day, his bank balance caught his eye. Historically, even a slight sales increase had been accompanied by increasing chaos and conflict, so it was easy to miss. But, in the last few months, production had been calm and issue free. In fact, Matthew's only involvement with production had been sitting in on daily twenty-minute work-in-progress meetings and briefing the team on new jobs he had won. The impressive number at the bottom of Matthew's bank statement was a consequence of the steady trickle of new accounts that he had won, in conjunction with a slight uplift in existing customers' repeat-purchasing activity.

It's now clear to Matthew that Influx will have to grow significantly before the addition of a dedicated salesperson can be justified. In fact, Matthew has pushed that date further into the future by fine-tuning Influx's engagement model and substituting web conferences for standard field appointments. He travels now only to perform structured workshops—and Influx charges for these!

Rules Are (Sometimes) for Breaking

It's convenient to formulate lists of rules and use these for guidance when implementing SPE—rules such as *salespeople should work inside or outside, never both*. I've avoided the temptation to present lists of rules in this book, but it's only natural that readers will generate their own. And that's generally okay.

In most cases, rules like this will serve you well, but there are occasions on which greater flexibility is required. And, on these occasions, it's critical that you distinguish between rules (which are flexible) and principles (which are not).

Madison Inc. builds metalworking machines, primarily for the Detroit auto industry. Like many of our silent revolutionaries, Madison is a quiet achiever. It's a long-established, solidly profitable, midsize enterprise. After its founder first discovered SPE, some five years earlier, Madison had been gradually increasing sales volumes, primarily by stripping nonsales tasks away from salespeople.

A year ago, Madison's three salespeople's responsibilities had been reduced to the extent that they reasonably could be cut back, but—thanks to the addition of some new production technology—the sales team was not quite capable of selling all of Madison's production capacity.

Adding another salesperson was out of the question. Madison simply couldn't scale production fast enough to justify a 30-percent increase in the size of its sales team. And because Madison's salespeople were all engineers, with years of hands-on experience, the addition of a salesperson was an expensive commitment in terms of money and effort.

At this point, management convened a meeting with the salespeople to discuss the SPE inside sales application. This application seemed to make a lot of sense for Madison, because their three salespeople spent a lot of time inside anyway. It was clear to management that if the salespeople specialized in working either inside or outside, as opposed to the current mix, that would result in a significant increase in their productivity.

As is typically the case at Madison meetings, the team spent the first fifteen minutes in silence, reading (or rereading) a paper that described the SPE inside-out approach and the inside sales application. In the ensuing discussion, the salespeople unanimously agreed that the inside sales application made perfect sense. It was beyond question that productivity could be increased significantly if two of the current sales teams became dedicated inside salespeople and if the remaining one became a field specialist.

Although all of the salespeople agreed unreservedly that this direction made sense, they were each adamant that they did not personally want to work in this environment. None of the salespeople was prepared to be in the field full time, and none was happy with the idea of losing fieldwork altogether.

In a larger organization, it's unlikely that management would allow organizational design to be determined by the preferences of three individuals, but Madison is not a large organization, and management understood that a model that senior team members were not excited about was a model that simply wouldn't survive contact with reality.

In most cases, I advise that team members in general (not just salespeople) should work either inside or outside—and not a mix of the two. This is because the methods of operation for the two environments are quite different. If a team member is working inside, tasks (e.g., phone calls) can be queued upstream from them, and they can process task after task. This is not the case if the same person is operating in the field. Most field activities (e.g., appointments) need to be scheduled in a calendar, and the start time of each activity needs to be protected (e.g., by a gap following the preceding activity). Furthermore, because both field appointment durations and travel time are highly variable, a significant amount of safety buffer is required to protect a day's worth of field activities. This is one of the reasons that inside salespeople can easily have thirty meaningful selling conversations a day and field salespeople will top-out at four.

Because these modes of operation are quite different, salespeople struggle to transition between them. Specifically, when salespeople come inside after a spell in the field, it is very difficult for them to increase their rate of work ninefold to match the dedicated inside salesperson. Without tight supervision, salespeople who perform a mix of inside and outside work will end up performing just a handful of meaningful selling conversations when they're inside. This is not because they are lazy or ill intentioned; it's just because they're—well—people!

Interestingly, the Madison team discussed this very point. The salespeople agreed that this observation of human nature certainly applied to them. They agreed that occasional field visits took an enormous toll on their productivity, even after they returned to the office. In fact, they were relieved to discover that this was normal. They joked that at last they had evidence that engineers were human too!

Although it's generally preferable that a team member work inside or out and not both, we already know that this is not an absolute. Project leaders, for example, work both inside and out, and in the case of Influx (our small-business SPE application), we had Matthew (the CEO) performing a mix as well. In both of these cases, it is excusable, because we are not trying to maximize the individuals' productivity. A project leader should have plenty of protective capacity, and, similarly, it would not be wise to try to schedule a CEO at 100-percent utilization.

So, if the *inside or outside* rule can be broken in those cases, how about Madison's?

The Madison team understood clearly that the source of the productivity improvements they were pursuing was the division of labor. They recognized that the primary benefit of the division of labor came from specialization, and they also understood that there were two ways to get a person to specialize: You could allocate this person only one particular type of work, or you could batch together activities of the same type within time blocks.

Although this latter approach looked like a *get out of jail free* card, the Madison team was cautious. They could see that these time blocks would have to be large enough to really exploit the benefits of specialization, and they could also see that an arrangement like this would have to be policed; otherwise, it would rapidly devolve into their status quo.

Madison's ultimate resolutions were that salespeople could perform both inside and field tasks if—and only if—the minimum-size time block was one week (not one day), and if all field activities (other than visits), along with the planning of field trips, would be performed by someone other than salespeople. These resolutions lead naturally to the application shown in figure 29.

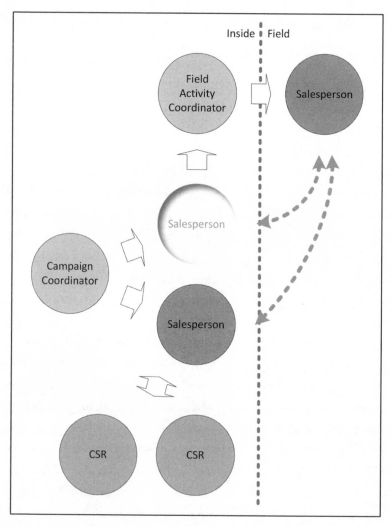

Figure 29. In the Madison application, inside salespeople periodically perform one-week field trips, scheduled and managed by field-activity coordinators.

The Madison application looks just like the inside sales application, except that the inside salespeople periodically venture outside to perform field trips. These trips have a minimum duration of one week.

What's critical, however, is that the salespeople have nothing to do with the scheduling or management of field trips. It's the responsibility of the field-activity coordinator to organize each trip, to ensure that the salespeople's calendars are booked solid for the duration of each trip (four meetings a day), and to perform all CRM data-entry and support activities while the salesperson is in the field.

Each trip is scheduled weeks in advance, and, in the lead-up to each trip, salespeople flag customers (and potential customers) they would like to visit. This structure ensures that when the salespeople are inside, they have thirty meaningful conversations a day (every day). But when they hang up their headsets and venture out, they are performing a solid four meetings a day for the duration of their time in the field

The Madison team—both management and the salespeople—love this model.

Madison added two field-activity coordinators, and those coordinators work together to ensure that each trip is solidly booked. The two field-activity coordinators are less expensive than an additional salesperson would have been, and the coordinators were up and running within their first week on the job. The result is that the sales team is significantly more productive than it previously was, and the volume of meaningful selling interactions has increased markedly for both inside and outside work.

Although the salespeople do work harder, their work is less stressful, because they no longer feel like they are multitasking. When a salesperson is on a field trip, their office-bound colleagues look after their open opportunities for them. And when they return, the field appointments they performed have resulted in many new opportunities that have been created and updated by the field-activity coordinators.

❀ ❀ ❀ ❀

It should be clear that each of these models is a derivation of our four key principles. Hopefully, now, you're ready to adopt—or customize—one of the applications we've discussed for your sales function. We're almost ready to launch into part 2 of the book, where we'll explore the practical implications of SPE.

However, before we do, we have one more sacred cow to confront. It's time to declare war on sales commissions, targets, and other artificial management stimulants.

Chapter 7
THE END OF COMMISSIONS, BONUSES, AND OTHER ARTIFICIAL MANAGEMENT STIMULANTS

If it's true that *sacred cows make the best hamburgers*, we're in for quite a feast!

I've chosen to close part one of this book with a frontal assault on the juiciest bovine of all: the unassailable belief that salespeople should be paid commissions. And while I'm at it, I'll take aim at bonuses, targets, and other artificial management stimulants.

A LITMUS TEST

This discussion is important for two reasons. First, commissions and their bedfellows will definitely handicap the performance of the reengineered sales environment I've gone to great lengths to describe. Second, this discussion will force us to confront the significant implications of sales process engineering (SPE), both locally and organization-wide.

If you are brave enough to follow in the footsteps of our silent revolutionaries, it's critical that you truly appreciate the *essence* of SPE. It's not enough to believe that SPE will work; you must also understand—at the most fundamental level—exactly *why* it will work. And if you don't, it almost certainly won't!

So I'm proposing that you use the emotionally charged question of salespeople's commissions as a kind of litmus test. If, by the end of this chapter, you are comfortable that there is no place for commissions in a reengineered sales environment, it's safe for you to proceed.

If, however, this conclusion still does not sit comfortably with you, it makes more sense to treat this book as an exercise in creative thinking—and to leave your sales function well alone.

WHEN COMMISSIONS MAKE SENSE

At its most fundamental level, SPE involves the transitioning of the responsibility for sales from autonomous agents to a centrally coordinated team. When sales is *actually* performed by autonomous agents, it does make sense to pay these agents on a commission basis, a percentage of the revenue they generate.

So, if we imagine a computer hardware manufacturer that sells desktop and notebook computers to consumers via big-box retailers, it's clear that these arm's-length retailers should be paid on a commission basis. And if we think about this example, we can identify two conditions that accord well with commission-based pay: These retail agents sell from stock—meaning that there is no requirement for them to interact with the hardware manufacturer on a transaction-by-transaction basis, which certainly would not be the case in an engineer-to-order environment, and these retail agents are *truly* autonomous—they march to their own drumbeats, and they own the relationship with the ultimate customer.

But what happens to the case for commission-based pay when these conditions are *not* in place? As we discussed in chapter 2, when we transition from a make-to-stock to an engineer-to-order environment, the case for autonomy becomes weaker. Increasingly, the performance of the organization as a whole becomes more a function of the quality of integration between sales and production. And, because *autonomy* and *teamwork* are polar opposites, as the case for autonomy becomes weaker, we reach a point at which we have to make a clean switch from one to the other—there's simply no such thing as an autonomous team member!

The Wrong Question

We now arrive at the critical question. We should not begin this discussion by asking whether commissions make sense; rather, we should ask whether we should sell via autonomous agents or via a centrally coordinated team.

Once we answer this question, our position on commissions becomes obvious.

THE CASE AGAINST COMMISSIONS

In order to understand why, let's briefly revisit the history of manufacturing. There was a time (before the industrial revolution) when almost all labor was paid on a piece rate. Piece-rate pay is the manufacturing equivalent of a commission. Rather than being paid in units of time, a piece-rate worker is paid according to their units of output. A stitcher, for example, might receive twenty cents for each garment processed.

Today, however, piece-rate pay is almost extinct. (And, I suspect by now, you have a good idea why!) What happened is management discovered that, as the complexity of the environment increased, there was a critical threshold beyond which scheduling decisions had to be made centrally. Of course, beyond this threshold, piece-rate pay had to be eliminated because it drove workers to work as fast as possible and not to subordinate to the schedule. Remember, because of the combination of *dependency* and *variability*, you never maximize the output of a system by maximizing the rate-of-work of each system resource.

Commissions (or any kind of performance pay) are inappropriate in the reengineered sales environments described in this book for exactly the same reason that piece-rate pay is now inappropriate in manufacturing environments.

And this conclusion does not apply just to the sales function in isolation. As we discussed in chapter 4, in many organizations, it is not healthy for sales to be the organizational constraint. So, in these cases, irrespective of the structure of the sales function, the organization as a whole will perform better when sales is *not* operating at 100-percent utilization.

I wish this could be my last word on that subject. However, there are a number of persistent objections to my position that we must first put to bed. First, an organization might say they have a mixed environment: salespeople are not fully autonomous—meaning that a mix of salary and commissions is justified. The second objection is even if we don't need the compensation plan to determine salespeople's rate of work, we still need performance pay to maximize salespeople's quality of work (in other words, without commissions, what would motivate salespeople to actually sell?). A third would be that commissions enable us to mitigate against the uncertain nature of salespeople's performance and keep costs under control. And, finally, the theory may make sense, but good salespeople will simply not be prepared to work in an environment without commissions.

The Fallacy of a Mixed Environment

I've heard many executives argue that it's beneficial for their salespeople to be partially autonomous, but I've never heard anyone argue that it's beneficial for salespeople to be partial team members. Perhaps that is because the latter phrasing exposes the folly of this position.

I've already stressed that it is impossible for salespeople to be team members and autonomous agents at the same time. However, an astute reader might argue that this is possible in theory (if not in practice). Your salespeople can be capable team members and operate autonomously if (and only if) the rest of the organization has the capacity to subordinate to individual salespeople.

At first glance, this condition may not appear to be particularly onerous. However, when we consider the enormous variability in salespeople's output, we recognize that effective subordination would require a huge amount of redundancy in customer service, engineering, and production. Remember, we're considering true *sales* here, not repeat *transactions*.

The fact that this is commercially unrealistic tends not to stop management from pursuing a mixed sales environment, and the consequences are as unpleasant as they are predictable: Management encourages salespeople to operate autonomously. Salespeople proceed from the assumption that more sales is always better (they figure the rest of the organization will keep up somehow). On average, the sales team as a whole may well sell less than the organization has the capacity to produce. However, because new accounts are won infrequently, the load on the rest of the organization is irregular. On the occasions that customer service, engineering, or production does not have the capacity to honor the (often optimistic) commitments made by salespeople, on-time performance is compromised and salespeople attempt to placate upset customers with even more optimistic promises. The resulting chaos reduces the organization's effective production capacity.

Periodically, management attempts to improve the financial performance of the organization with additional incentives and special promotions. Finally, these incentives tend to increase the lumpiness of the deal flow— meaning that, over time, peak sales increase at the expense of average sales.

The bottom line is that contradictions cannot persist indefinitely. Your salespeople cannot be both autonomous agents and team members. They cannot be responsible only for sales outcomes and simultaneously be expected to attend sales meetings and maintain the organization's customer relationship management application (CRM). And customers cannot belong to both salespeople and to your organization.

Commissions and the Quality of Work

If salespeople don't have the opportunity to earn a commission, why would they sell? I wish I had a dollar for every time that I've been asked this question by an incredulous executive. You would think the onus should be on the defender of performance pay to present an argument. After all, receptionists answer the phone when it rings, in spite of the fact that they receive no incremental pay. Your financial controller does a good job of paying bills on time, in spite of the fact that they receive no rebate on each check signed. And even senior executives perform important tasks, absent special incentives (I'm assuming that no one is paying you to read this book!). Why should salespeople differ from almost every other worker on the planet?

The answer is simple: They shouldn't. Absent the opportunity to earn a commission, salespeople will still sell *because they are salespeople.*

I often wonder whether those executives who ask that question are really inquiring into the motivation of their team members or whether they are providing an (unsolicited) insight into their own pathology.

In *Drive*, his excellent best seller, Daniel Pink presents a powerful case against performance pay. His conclusion—backed up by many experiments from the social sciences—is that external rewards retard the performance of knowledge workers and have positive effects only in situations in which the workers are performing mindless, repetitive tasks.

In other words, if your team members are responsible for activities any more complex than licking stamps, the work itself is their reward. Pink's conclusion points to an interesting defense of performance pay in the traditional sales environment.

Consider these two points: In most environments, the volume of sales appointments has a far greater influence on sales output than the qualitative performance of the salesperson, and in almost all environments, salespeople generate their own opportunities as a result of mindless and repetitive prospecting activities. With these points in mind, commissions may be defensible in traditional sales environments, not because they motivate salespeople to sell, but because they motivate them to prospect!

Of course, in our case, this argument is moot, because we are definitely going to free salespeople of the requirement to generate their own sales opportunities.

Commissions as a Hedge against Nonperformance

The obvious problem with the argument that performance pay provides management with a hedge against the costs associated with salespeople's nonperformance is that the same argument could be applied to everyone in the organization. But, then sales *is* a special case for a couple of reasons: First, the performance of salespeople is highly variable, and second, it is easy to isolate the contribution that a salesperson makes (this would not be so easy, e.g., in the case of a line worker).

As we'll discuss momentarily, SPE negates these two reasons: The output of the sales function ceases to be highly variable, and it becomes difficult—if not impossible—to isolate the contribution that a salesperson's activity makes to the organization as a whole.

First, however, let's consider the wider (and more terrifying) implications of performance pay.

On Management Abdication

I mentioned earlier that you cannot manage an autonomous agent; these two concepts are antagonistic. Performance pay makes this contradiction explicit. In other words, when a significant component of a salesperson's pay is performance-based, management has formally abdicated its responsibility for sales. In so doing, management has telegraphed to salespeople that selling is *optional!* It is now up to individual salespeople whether they generate sales—and in what quantity.

If a salesperson is capable of selling, the real cost of their nonperformance is not their salary; it's the profits that the organization does not earn when production is sitting idle. If a salesperson is *not* capable of selling, the real cost of their nonperformance is *still* not their salary; it's the sales opportunities that are lost but that could have been won if they were attended to by a more capable individual.

Variability Diminished

If selling conversations are the primary driver of sales (and it's rare that they are not), management can significantly reduce the variability of sales by taking control of the volume of sales conversations performed by the team as a whole. As the volume of meaningful selling interactions increases, the variability of the entire sales function will reduce.[9]

Of course, the inside-out model achieves this by ensuring that salespeople perform *nothing* other than selling conversations and by ensuring that each salesperson performs ten times the volume of appointments they would perform in a typical sales environment.

The Salesperson's Capability

Many of our silent revolutionaries report an increase in salespeople's capability. There are three contributing factors here:

1. Selection: If organizations reduce the size of their sales teams, they obviously retain their more capable salespeople.
2. Practice: When salespeople do nothing other than sell, they get good at it, or they rapidly conclude that sales is not the right career for them.
3. Feedback: With control over salespeople—and with accurate and current data—sales management can provide salespeople with a faster and more accurate performance feedback.

Salespeople's Position on Commissions

If there's one thing I've learned in the last ten years or so, it's that sales managers are uniformly terrible at predicting their salespeople's reaction to the inside-out model. Almost without exception, sales managers predict outrage from their team members—perhaps even a mass exodus of talent. And the one component of our model that sales managers predict will be the most offensive is the elimination of commissions.

In reality, salespeople's reaction to this proposition tends to be shocking for exactly the opposite reason. It's shocking how comfortable they are to give up both their autonomy and their variable compensation plan.

The reason salespeople tend to be so compliant is very simple. Salespeople—contrary to popular opinion—do not live in a parallel universe. They are a part of the same dysfunctional reality that causes the rest of the organization (including management) so much pain. Salespeople may have different theories about the source of their particular set of issues—and they may propose different initiatives as a remedy to these issues—but, when presented with the evidence, they recognize (often faster than management does) that a significant number of sales problems, production problems, and management problems can be tracked back to the same root cause: their autonomous mode of operation.

And make no mistake—salespeople have more than their fair share of complaints. They hate the volume of clerical and customer service work that prevents them from engaging meaningfully with potential and existing customers. They don't enjoy spending their evenings in hotels, entering data in the CRM, generating expense reports, and writing proposals. They resent the continual conflict over the allocation of commissions—particularly when accounts span multiple territories. They hate having to advise customers that their promises will not be met, and they resent the fact that they have to live with the continuous uncertainty over production performance. And they don't enjoy the underlying—and constant—conflict in their relationships with production, customer service, engineering, management, and even finance.

It may be true that salespeople are in love with the notion of the salesperson as a lone crusader, but they are also realists. They quickly recognize that, on balance, the proposed environment will be infinitely more rewarding to work in. Sure, they sacrifice their autonomy, but so what? They each get a dedicated executive assistant (the business-development coordinator), who will free them to do nothing but sell. And sure, they have to transition from commissions to a salary, but what of it? Salespeople understand that the dynamics of the environment in which they operate rob them of the financial upside they signed on for. And, the truth be known, salespeople have never been entirely comfortable with the notion that they are innately lazy, prepared only to do the right thing on the promise of an incremental financial inducement.

THE NEW COMPENSATION PLAN

So, it's out with commissions and in with a new compensation plan. And there's not much to the new plan. The idea is simple: We pay people what they are worth (and perhaps a little more).

That's it!

In practice, you should pay salespeople enough to ensure that compensation is no longer a regular topic of conversation, and then insist that they perform the activities required for the organization to achieve its objectives.

So here, from management's perspective, are the fundamental differences between the two compensation plans: With performance pay, we make optimal performance optional, and then we attempt to exert control through a compensation plan that underlines salespeople's autonomy with every paycheck. And with salaries, we take the discussion of money off the table. Salespeople willingly subordinate to a central schedule, and they perform necessary activities because they are asked to and because those activities are congruent with both their job descriptions and the reasonable interests of the organization.

This new plan, then, is not even new: It's exactly the same plan we use to compensate everyone else in the organization!

And when it comes to calculating salespeople's salaries, there are no surprises here either. As with all employees, there are two considerations: Replacement cost (how much would you have to pay for another person with a comparable set of capabilities?) and asking price (how much will you have to pay the current candidate to ensure that the compensation plan is no longer a regular topic of conversation?).

It should go without saying that it would be foolish to propose that salespeople (or any team members, for that matter) take a cut in pay when you transition to the inside-out model. Most of our silent revolutionaries shift their salespeople to a salary that is equal to or slightly greater than their average total earnings (typically judged over a three-year period).

If you think about it, both parties are getting a terrific deal here. Salespeople receive a not-insignificant increase in pay. Remember, even if you fix the salesperson's pay at their current average earnings, that's still a pay increase (a bird in the hand is worth two in the bush). And management increases the volume of effective work performed by each salesperson tenfold. To achieve the same increase in a typical sales environment, management would have to add nine more salespeople for every one they currently employ.

OTHER ARTIFICIAL MANAGEMENT STIMULANTS

This debate about commissions is like the Hydra (the many-headed monster). You successfully lop off one head and another appears. I fear that, even if I've done a reasonable job of convincing you that there's no place for commissions in the reengineered environment, your very next question might be *but what about bonuses?*

My observation is that bonus plans have a couple of problems. Because the bonus is remote from the positive behaviors that drive the desired outcome, the first installment of a bonus is a pleasant surprise, and subsequent installments are viewed as entitlements. Bonuses suggest to team members that they are responsible for outcomes when, in fact, managers should own this responsibility. Accordingly, bonuses tend to disempower managers.

It is certainly true that some degree of variability is required where compensation is concerned. However, my position is that standard salaries provide the necessary flexibility. As your team members become more capable, their market value increases, meaning that you are obliged to grant them pay increases when—or, ideally, before—they request them.[10]

I maintain that there is absolutely nothing wrong with the traditional contract between employers and employees. Employees want to be able to perform rewarding work in a secure environment. If they were really seeking uncertainty and the potential for boundless riches, they would not have signed on to be employees in the first place.

The other stimulants (e.g., targets and quotas) are problematic for the same reasons as commissions and bonuses: They tend to suggest that team members own outcomes. In a team environment, the team cannot own the responsibility for anything. There is no collective consciousness—only a group of individuals. It is critical, therefore, that the manager own the responsibility for the desired outcome and that team members own the responsibility only for the activities assigned to them.

Here, a military example is illuminating. Imagine if, rather than allocating discrete responsibilities to each of his units, a commander were simply to assemble all his troops and exhort them to take Baghdad!

REINVENTING MANAGEMENT

On the subject of management, it's important to recognize that the transition to a reengineered sales environment is extremely difficult for sales managers. If sales managers were to refer to a list they had compiled before the transition of everything they know for sure about sales, almost every statement on that list would be false after the transition. Consequently, it is not sufficient to reengineer the general sales environment. You must also rebuild from scratch the sales manager's method of operation.

❈ ❈ ❈ ❈

You now have a sound understanding of the theory that underpins sales process engineering. Part 2 of this book will show you how to convert all this theory into practice.

Part 2

PUTTING IT ALL TOGETHER

Chapter 8
FORMULATING A PLAN

Here's where we dot all the *i*'s and cross all the *t*'s. We'll be talking about roles, workflows, campaigns, technology, and much more, but I don't think we should be satisfied with examining these building blocks in isolation, or in a vacuum. After all, part 2 is all about practice, not theory. Accordingly, it's my intention to weave a conversation about how these building blocks will fit together, and in what sequence they should be deployed.

It's important, therefore, that we set the scene for this conversation. What we need to get started is a high-level plan. You need a model for your new environment, you need a rough understanding of the resourcing and cost implications of the inside-out model, and you need to know what the transition is likely to look like.

Interestingly, without guidance, most executives approach these questions in the opposite order. They start planning the transition without a clear understanding of the model or its resourcing implications. As a consequence, a recent convert to our cause tends to be preoccupied with questions like the following: Do we start with salespeople, perhaps? Provide them new job descriptions and a revised compensation plan? Do we start with promotions? More sales opportunities will never go astray, right? Or do we start with technology? After all, there's something cathartic about a new enterprise application and all the friendly consultants who come live with us during its implementation. Of course, all of these approaches are wrong—dangerously wrong!

A plan that commences with these initiatives will almost certainly fail. Worse still, it will fail so spectacularly that it will discredit the whole notion of sales process engineering (SPE)—providing you with little choice but to persist with the traditional model, despite its shortcomings.

THE MODEL

As I suggested above, the identification of the ideal model is the starting point. If one of the applications described in part 1 is a perfect fit, that's terrific. Otherwise, you have three choices:

1. Simplify your environment to fit one of the existing applications.
2. Combine two or more of the existing applications (as per the *inside-out model*).
3. Either customize or create your own application.

You should be hesitant to use the complexity of your current environment as a reason for creating a new application. More often than not, I discover that complexity destroys value, rather than creating it.

Here's a model created by PolyArts, one of our silent revolutionaries. PolyArts manufactures plastic sheeting and also has a division that fabricates sheeting into custom product packaging and point-of-sale displays.

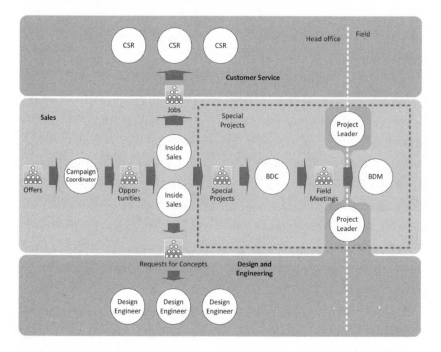

Figure 30. Sales and customer service model for a manufacturer of sheet plastics and fabricated packaging materials.

At first glance, this model looks a little more complicated than the diagrams we encountered in part 1, but if you look a little closer, you'll realize that what we're dealing with here is the inside-out model, just with a little more detail.

PolyArts included their design team because either drawings or prototypes are required for most packaging proposals. They adjusted the number of circles to represent the number of people they have in each role, and they added little queues of works in progress to indicate the key metrics they intended to monitor.

A diagram like this is very valuable, for a couple of reasons. First, the best way to plan a change like this is to have your team create a model in this form; and second, it's a great communication tool: You'll find that your existing team members will understand a diagram like figure 30 at a glance.

Creating Your Model

The best way to arrive at a model like that of PolyArts is to follow the process described in chapter 4. In other words, start inside and work outward. For this discussion, we'll assume you're adopting the inside-out model.

Customer Service

Specifically, start with a blank sheet of paper and add a number of circles to represent your customer service team.

Now, here's a warning! This process will be very painful and unproductive if you are considering your team members at the same time that you are formulating a design for your new model. You need to forget about your existing team members for the moment. I often counsel executives to pretend that their entire sales and customer service team has gone missing for some unimaginable reason and that they must rebuild this function from scratch.

Ultimately, it'll be easier to convince your team members to get behind a model that looks like it will work than it will to excite them with the sorry result of compromise and equivocation (even if the new model requires that they make uncomfortable changes).

You should add enough customer service representatives to cope with your existing volume of orders, quote requests, and issues—even if your salespeople are currently responsible for some (or all) of these activities.

This, of course, is because soon enough they will not be.

You should also ensure that your customer service team is large enough to provide you with sufficient protective capacity. You need this for a few reasons:

Customer service tasks need to be processed quickly. Orders should be entered within minutes of their receipt, and quote requests and issues should be processed within single-digit hours (not days!). Believe me, your customers will reward you for this—with more orders.

The inbound flow of work is quite variable. You need to resource for times of peak load, not for your average load.

Your capacity is even more variable. For example, if you have a team of five customer service representatives (CSRs) and one has a day off, you have just lost 20 percent of your capacity. It's quite likely that you can't afford for your lead-times to blow out by a commensurate amount.

On the subject of variability and protective capacity, you should be looking to build *one* customer service team—as opposed to multiple teams, perhaps in different locations. This is because a single team enables you to pool both supply and demand—meaning that you need a smaller team to provide you with the same amount of protective capacity.

If you do have operators in different locations, I would strongly encourage you to incorporate them into one *virtual* team. A few of our silent revolutionaries have permanent video feeds, so the CSRs in each location can see all their remote colleagues in real time.

Inside Sales and Campaign Coordination

It's time to add some more circles now to represent your inside sales team, and if you have an inside sales team (or a sales team of any type, for that matter) you'll need sales opportunities. Opportunities come from campaigns of various kinds, so that means you need a campaign coordinator too.

So, you've just added a minimum of two more circles.

"But what," I can hear you asking, "if we don't need an inside sales team?" It's possible—but unlikely—that this is the case. For this to be true you would have to confirm that your existing salespeople spend next to no time on their phones (or email) selling and that your customers are not interested in having meaningful selling conversations via any medium other than face to face. If you can honestly confirm that these are true for your organization, you have my permission to skip ahead!

To determine how many inside salespeople you need, calculate how many meaningful selling interactions your entire existing sales team has in an average day. Multiply that by four, because quadrupling your daily selling interactions will be easily achievable with specialization. Then divide the result by thirty, which is the number of meaningful selling interactions that a dedicated inside salesperson should average. This is the number of inside salespeople you should start with, unless it is less than two—in which case, you should have two inside salespeople.

Two inside salespeople should be the minimum because if you have only one, it's hard to know whether to attribute results (or the lack thereof) to your process or to the capabilities of that person; and because if you don't currently have an inside sales team, you are likely to have some turnover in your first few months while you are building this function.

Unless you're doing more than about $100 million in annual sales, you'll need only one campaign coordinator. This is because your campaign coordinator always processes opportunities in batches, and thanks to technology, those batch sizes can increase significantly without requiring much additional effort.

In many—nearly all—cases, you'll want to add one or more research analysts to your promotions team. These people are responsible for doing the online and telephone research required to compile lists for your campaign coordinator. It is possible, I know, to purchase lists, but in most cases, these lists will still require additional research to be useful. Most of our silent revolutionaries commission work-from-home contractors to fill these roles.

Field Specialists

If you do need people in the field, you now need to carefully consider the nature and volume of activities these people will be performing.

For the nature of these activities, you can divide field visits into three categories:

1. purely technical visits or technical sales visits (e.g., demonstrations, technical requirement discovery, or troubleshooting),
2. transactional sales (e.g., dropping by to take an order), and
3. enterprise sales (e.g., running solution-design workshops, presenting to groups of decision makers).

Of these three activities, the first two are not really sales in a business-development sense, but that's not to say that they are not necessary. The first is critical, simply because there are some sales related activities that must be performed on location, and, in some organizations, there is some requirement for the second because, sadly, there are still customers who insist you visit them periodically to take an order.

What should be clear, however, is that you do not need to recruit an enterprise-class salesperson to perform these activities. In fact, in many cases, you're better off with a technical person with solid people skills than you are with a pure salesperson.

As you know, my preference is to allocate the activities of those first two types to field specialists, who are—you guessed it—technical people with solid people skills. To calculate how many circles you need to represent your field specialists, determine the average number of daily field meetings your team performs that are genuinely required and that fit into those first two categories, then divide that number by four, the daily capacity of a field specialist.

Now, if your math tells you that you need fewer field specialists than you expect, please resist the temptation to stare at the number in disbelief and then revise it upward based purely on your intuition. Executives are incredulous when the numbers suggest that they can manage with a field force one-fifth of its current size, as is often the case. The common response is, *we just have to have more boots on the ground than that!*

What you must remember is that the crucial point here is not the number of field representatives you employ; it's *how much time* they spend face to face with customers. If all those designer boots spend most of their time parked in the salespeople's home offices, your customers are deriving no incremental benefit from them. Remember, your math allows for exactly the same number of field meetings you currently have—in addition to a significant increase in other forms of contact.

You'll remember from chapter 4 that field specialists perform discrete tasks that are allocated to them by inside salespeople and sometimes by customer service representatives. To begin, you can give your inside sales and customer service teams direct access to the field specialists' calendars.

As your team grows, you may find that the scheduling complexity increases to the point where you want to have a dedicated field scheduler who receives visit requests from the inside sales and customer service teams and then plans the field specialists' routes for them. This is certainly the case if you have field specialists covering large geographic areas.

If you go down this path, remember that a field scheduler is quite different from a business-development coordinator. The former is a dispatch operator; the latter is essentially an executive assistant.

When the time comes, this decision (and other similar ones) is easy to make. Assume a team of five inside salespeople, each with the ability to generate $3,000 a day in sales. If you can observe that scheduling field visits reduces inside salespeople's effective capacity by 20 percent, it's pretty easy to build a solid case for adding a field scheduler.

In case you're wondering, the PolyArts model above does not feature field specialists. Because their requirement for field-specialist activities was relatively low, they elected to push these activities to project leaders instead.

Business Development

Most organizations have a requirement for some field-based, business-development activities: the enterprise-sales activities mentioned above (e.g., running solution-design workshops, presenting to groups of decision makers). But the high-value opportunities that spawn these activities are few and far between. These high-value opportunities tend to be lumped in with the higher-volume, more-transactional ones—meaning they don't get the attention they deserve.

As before, you first need to determine how many enterprise field activities you perform today across your team as a whole. Then you can double that number and divide the result by twenty. That will tell you the number of business-development managers (BDMs) you need and the number of business-development coordinators (BDCs) you need to pair them with (remembering that there's always a one-to-one relationship between BDMs and BDCs). Here, we're planning to double your existing volume of business-development activity. It's reasonable to expect that this additional volume will be a natural consequence of your additional inside sales activity. You should not, however, plan for any more enterprise activity than this. It's highly unlikely that your promotions team will have the capacity to focus on generating enterprise opportunities for quite some time.

You will almost certainly be surprised by how few BDMs you need, and that's a good thing. It's better to have fewer and spend the money to get high-caliber people in this role. Typically, our silent revolutionaries have one BDM for every $30 million in annual sales (give or take).

Now, if your organization's not big enough to generate twenty field-based business-development activities a week, you should not have any BDMs. Instead, members of your senior executive team should perform these meetings.

A lot of smaller organizations use this requirement as an excuse to employ an executive assistant for the chief executive. The executive assistant fills the role of sales coordinator until the organization can justify making this a full-time role, and they easily pay for themselves, because they multiply the productivity of the senior executive across their entire range of responsibilities.

Project Leaders

As we discussed in chapter 3, it's critical that project leaders partner with BDMs to prosecute opportunities on the far side of the complexity threshold. You'll remember that project leaders prevent BDMs from becoming entangled in projects in some technical and most engineer-to-order environments.

My experience is that the idea of project leadership is a very easy sell in those organizations in which it makes sense. This is because salespeople's entanglement in projects, after a sale, does so much damage and for so many parties that executives can't wait to fix the problem once they understand its cause!

This means that if you're not sure you need project leaders, you probably don't. If you have only an occasional deal that needs project leadership, you can probably blend this role with that of the field specialist.

However, if you know that you need project leaders, it's important that you don't skimp on this critical role. In your case, project leadership is like customer service, in that you must maintain protective capacity. If you don't, BDMs will be forced to get entangled in project management, which will violate your standard workflows and set your BDMs at odds with their BDCs.

You'll be shocked at how quickly a lack of project-leadership capacity can cause a beautifully functioning complex sales environment to devolve back into its less beautiful and less functional, pre-SPE state! For this reason, you must ensure that your project leadership team has the capacity to handle more projects than your BDMs have the capacity to sell. And on the occasion that you run out of project-leadership capacity, you must ensure that your BDMs stop work on opportunities that require project leadership.

Unfortunately, there's no rule of thumb to inform you of the number of project leaders you require. The one thing I can say with certainty is that you need more project leaders than BDMs. If you genuinely need project leaders, you'll certainly need between two and four for each of your BDMs.

To estimate the correct number, you should map a workflow for prosecuting a representative sales opportunity—right though to production or project team hand-off: Estimate the time commitment for both the BDM and the project leader in quarter-day blocks; estimate the percentage of opportunities that progress to each milestone in this workflow and discount those time commitments appropriately; and finally, estimate the project leader's time commitment to projects after hand-off and add it to their presale commitment.

You'll probably discover that those opportunities you win end up consuming four to five times the number of project leaders' quarter-day time blocks relative to the BDMs' time blocks, but when you remember that only a tiny percentage of the opportunities you pursue will end up progressing all the way to deals, this will ease your requirement for project leaders somewhat—and, no doubt, your blood pressure!

If you have an engineering or a design team, your project leaders should be a part of that team and should be promoted from within that team. However, your project leaders must not be billable resources within that team.

Let me say that again. If you sell services on a time-and-materials basis, your project leaders *must not be billable resources.* In these environments, project leaders must be treated as an overhead expense. Otherwise, the pressure on the project leaders to bill will result in their being loaded to 100 percent utilization—meaning you no longer have protective capacity.

Work in Progress

If you glance back at PolyArts's model, you'll see a number of queues of work in progress (WIP) on the schematic. As is the case in production environments, the amount of WIP is our primary source of process-performance information. Specifically, in order to manage intelligently, we need to know

- how much WIP is in the process in total,
- how much WIP is at various locations within the process, and
- what the composition is of each queue of WIP.

In sales environments, it typically makes sense to measure WIP in days' worth of work (not hours or minutes). For example, our silent revolutionaries will typically make comments such as the following: "Our BDM has eight days of pending appointments." This means that if you count their forward-booked meetings and divide the result by their daily capacity, you'll find eight days of work in the queue.

Queue size takes on different significance depending on whether the downstream resource is the nominated constraint (in which case, they should be fully loaded) or a nonconstraint (in which case, they should have protective capacity).

So, in PolyArts's case, they want to ensure that queues of sales opportunities don't drop below their optimal size (inside sales is the system constraint); but they want to ensure that the queues upstream from customer service and design don't become too large.

We'll talk more about management in future chapters, but for now, it's worth considering the minimum number of points in your model at which you will need to measure queue size in order to have a good understanding of the status of the process as a whole.

Regional Offices

When PolyArts initially created their model, the process forced them to come face-to-face with the fact that they no longer needed regional offices. Not only did they not need them, but the transition to the inside-out model was also dependent on them closing regional offices.

Like many organizations, PolyArts had adopted a cellular approach to growth. They started with one location that made money and then grew by trying to replicate that office in multiple locations.

Except that isn't what actually happened. What they ended up with was one relatively efficient head-office operation and a number of incredibly inefficient regional offices. This is because none of the regional operations were large enough to harvest the economies of scale enjoyed in the head office. What's more, their distributed structure required that they add a

layer of management to keep the peace between the head office and each
of the regional offices. And I do mean *keep the peace*!

The thinking behind this cellular approach to growth was that it was
beneficial for salespeople to operate in close proximity to customers (as once
it was), it must also be beneficial to locate customer service, inventory, final
assembly, service, and other functions close to customers, too. PolyArts
quickly discovered the problem was that in most cases, it didn't make sense
to locate inventory and operational functions close to customers. It was
better to pool demand and let the resulting economies of scale offset the
higher transportation costs.

With minimal operational responsibilities, the regional locations became
what are commonly called *sales offices*. And, as PolyArts discovered, sales
offices tend not to be particularly good for sales, for a couple of reasons.
Senior salespeople—who should probably be BDMs—end up assuming the
role of general managers, and the other salespeople become almost totally
office bound, morphing into highly paid customer service representatives.

PolyArts was quick to recognize that activities that could be performed
in an office should be performed from the head office—and not from a
regional one. They also recognized that those people who are expected to
spend their time face-to-face with customers do not need access to an office.

The upshot was that PolyArts shuttered a handful of offices across
North America at the beginning of their transition to this new model.
Interestingly, the centralization of customer service and inside sales was a
boon for customers, because it put both these functions in close contact
with design and production—meaning that information quality went up
and that lead times went down. It was also well received by those field-based
personnel who happened to live in the regional locations. Their feedback
was that they much preferred dealing directly with the head office.

My general advice where sales offices are concerned is that you don't
need them. If you must have regional offices for operational reasons,
please make sure that your regionally based field personnel do not have
access to them.

In some cases, it can take quite a while to decommission regional offices. You might, for example, have talented team members who are incapable of moving. In those cases, as I suggested earlier, you should incorporate those regional team members into national (virtual) teams. This means that they answer to a national supervisor, attend daily WIP meetings with their national compatriots, and (ideally) wave to each other on giant monitors displaying video feeds from other offices (or from team members' home offices).

The Economics

You should now have a first draft of your resourcing model—something like PolyArts's diagram a few pages back. Before we proceed to planning your transition, we need to confirm that your proposed model makes economic sense. At a minimum, to pass this test, two conditions must be met:

1. The model, when it is implemented, must result in a significant increase in sales activity (meaningful selling interactions).
2. The model, when it is implemented, cannot cause an immediate increase in your organization's operating expenses.

Of these two conditions, the second one requires special attention.

It would appear that an increase in operating expenses is not universally bad. After all, if your volume of sales activity increases tenfold (or more), you could argue that a small increase in costs is justifiable.

The problem is that this argument ignores one very important point. Without question, your transition to the inside-out model will be complex, difficult, and—consequently—time consuming. It's simply impossible to make changes of this magnitude in a month or two. As we'll see shortly, the transition needs to progress in steps—with validation of each before progression to the next. In addition, the cycle time of the sales process as a whole—from the origination of a sales opportunity through the finalization of a sale can often be a number of months. Both factors impose a natural limit on the speed at which you can make decisions during the transition.

Another issue is that often the changes you want to make to the sales function require changes to be made elsewhere in the organization. It might be that more capacity is required in engineering or that your offerings require upgrades in order to make them more marketable. This means that if you allow operating expenses to increase on day one of your transition, you may have to wait many months before you see these additional expenses eclipsed by an increase in throughput.

Let me assure you that your transition will be difficult enough without the additional pressure of your financial controller (and skeptical board members) reminding you each month of the cumulative cost of your expensive little experiment!

If you do the math and discover that your model will result in an immediate increase in operating expenses, you have little choice but to reduce headcount. The mistake most managers make is to attempt to maintain a larger field sales team than is actually required. This deprives them of the budget required to build out the critical internal team—rendering a transition to the inside-out model impossible. Placing a cap on operating expenses will force you to be realistic about the size of your field team.

Of course, downsizing your field sales team does not mean laying off team members. The alternative is to transition field salespeople into other roles: Inside sales and project leader roles are the obvious candidates.

Remember, if you are decommissioning regional sales offices, you should take these savings into account in your calculations. Shuttering a regional sales office or two will give you enormous latitude where resourcing decisions are concerned. This is just one of the many reasons we love to decommission regional sales offices!

By the way, it's smart to reconsider the economics of your sales function at each stage in your transition, not just at the start. Specifically, it's wise to ensure at each step in your transition that sales activity increases (meaningful selling interactions) and that operating expenses do not increase by more than the increase in throughput you have generated to date.

THE TRANSITION: THE SEQUENCE IS EVERYTHING

Where planning your transition is concerned, the sequence is everything, and the sequence that works is exactly the opposite of the sequence that comes naturally to most managers. The key is to start at the factory door and work outward, toward the field—not to start with field representatives or promotional initiatives. If you don't have a factory, the principle is the same: Start as close to production as possible.

In real terms, this means that you start your transition by fortifying customer service—and engineering if you're an engineer-to-order environment. There are two reasons that it's important that you start here: You need a lot of additional capacity in customer service to cope with an increase in sales activity and to enable salespeople to offload the customer service tasks they are currently performing; and in most cases, you can generate immediate but small increases in sales just by reducing your customer service lead times (i.e., faster quotes, order processing, and issue resolution).

If you start elsewhere, pretty much anything you do will increase the load on customer service, and if your customer service team is underresourced and underskilled, as most are, this team will quickly become your bottleneck. Once this happens, customer service lead times will explode, customer satisfaction will drop, tempers around the organization will become frayed, and your improvement initiative will get itself a bad reputation right out of the gate!

Where you finish your transition is also important. Specifically, you should postpone making changes to your field salespeople until you absolutely have to, and when you do make changes, you should ensure that these changes are driven by the results you are generating with your internal activities.

Here's a concrete example: If you tell your field salespeople that you would like them to support your inside sales team, it's likely that they will be less than enthusiastic about this proposition. However, once the inside salespeople start to push discrete field activities to the salespeople's calendars, the field salespeople will quickly discover that they enjoy performing these activities and that they appreciate being able to move on to the next meeting with no requirement for data entry or routine follow up.

Now, that's not to say that you should keep field salespeople in the dark about what's happening. Communication is important, obviously. The point is that you should ask salespeople to maintain their existing modus operandi until your success with the internal components of the model force field changes on you.

Now that we agree on where to start and finish, let's work though each of the seven steps in a successful transition to SPE.

Step 1: Appoint a Project Champion

Someone has to champion a change (i.e., a project) of this magnitude—and *someone* is not a committee. The champion can be your VP of sales or even the owner of a smaller organization, or it can be an up-and-coming executive who's willing to take on this transition as a full-time special project.

The champion cannot be a typical sales manager; they are wedded to the orthodoxy. And it can't be a busy midlevel manager unless they resign all other responsibilities.

For our successful silent revolutionaries, their transitions to SPE were championed either by a senior executive (at the VP level or higher) or by an up-and-coming executive who dedicated himself to this project full time. There are no exceptions!

Step 2: Sell the New Direction

You should sell the new direction in two steps: a high-level overview for the organization as a whole, and then detailed briefings for each of the teams that will be affected directly by the transition.

You should make it clear that people's jobs are secure and that their feedback will be listened to—and that the model will be fine-tuned as data is collected. But you should also make it clear that the general direction is not negotiable and that the transition will not be derailed by the personal preferences of individuals.

If you are not confident that you can sell the transition with this kind of conviction, don't even consider starting on this journey.

Step 3: Take Control of Sales Activity Volume

Now, I know I said that you shouldn't touch field salespeople until as late as possible in your transition, but there's some basic housekeeping that's required before you get started.

As I mentioned previously, the primary antecedent of sales is sales activities: meaningful selling interactions. Whatever you do, you must ensure that your volume of meaningful selling interactions increases at each stage of your transition. Doing so reduces the risks in your transition.

This requires that you start your transition with an understanding of your current volume of meaningful selling interactions—your baseline. It's likely that you don't know that number right now, and even if you think you do, it's likely that the data in your customer relationship management application (CRM) misrepresents the truth.

To resolve this problem, you need to do three things immediately: First, you must insist that your existing salespeople start using your group calendar application to record all meaningful selling interactions. You can start by counting just the ones that are prescheduled, if you like; they tend to be the meaningful ones. Your sales manager should advise salespeople on exactly how they should record these interactions; it's often handy to color code them by activity type and to weight types according to the effort expended. Second, you must insist that your sales manager run weekly sales meetings if they aren't already, and that, in each meeting, they view each salesperson's calendar, count and record the number of meaningful selling interactions, and discuss with the salesperson—in front of the team—why the calendar looks the way it does. Finally, you must insist that your sales manager chart these numbers and communicate its contents to the leadership team on a weekly basis.

It's quite likely that your salespeople—and your sales manager—will not be overjoyed by these requirements. But, in my experience, you can enforce them in nearly all cases without causing mass defections. It's also been my experience that the act of discussing real meaningful selling interaction data with salespeople each week will cause your activity levels to rise without additional changes.

Step 4: Fix Customer Service

Now that you've sold the change and established a meaningful selling interaction baseline, it's time to roll up your sleeves and fix customer service. Inevitably, this will require that you add both people and capabilities to your customer service team. In addition to adding and training customer service representatives, you need to

- ensure that all work (order processing, quoting, and issue management) is performed in your enterprise resource planning (ERP) software (if you can't manage issues in ERP, you might have to use the CRM for this purpose);
- ensure that every activity (e.g., calls, emails, instant messaging sessions) is tracked in the same system in which the work is performed; and
- institute a daily stand-up WIP meeting, where open jobs are discussed and expediting decisions are made.

It makes a lot of sense to chart your on-time completion percentage for customer service work. As well as giving you a view of your current service levels, this chart will give you an understanding of the load on your team and—more important—the status of your necessary protective capacity.

You can deem your customer service team to be *fixed* when greater than 90 percent of work is processed within target lead times and when you maintain sufficient protective capacity to give you confidence that this number can be maintained indefinitely.

As you build your customer service capacity, you can encourage your sales manager to put gentle pressure on your field salespeople to route customer service tasks to your customer service team. Once your customers discover the existence of this customer service team, they'll quickly stop calling your field salespeople for transactional reasons.

Step 5: Build Inside Sales and Promotions

You need to build inside sales and promotions simultaneously. Remember that the job of inside sales is to prosecute sales opportunities, not to originate them. When you add inside sales, you will need to extract a couple more concessions from the field salespeople.

First, they will need to be prepared for the inside salespeople to push discrete field tasks to them. This will require that the field salespeople accurately maintain their calendars. It will also require that the field salespeople understand that when inside sales pushes a task to them, they are responsible for performing this task and reporting back to the inside salesperson who owns the overriding sales opportunity. In other words, the field salespeople will not take ownership of sales opportunities when they perform tasks for inside sales.

Second, the field salespeople will need to accept that accounts are now owned by the sales team as a whole, which is a polite way of saying that the notion of account ownership no longer really exists. This is important because you will want to ensure that both inside salespeople and field salespeople are calling on the same accounts, albeit with different propositions.

What you do not want to do is segment your accounts, allocating some to inside salespeople and some to field salespeople. This common approach will result in your best accounts being underserviced, and it will handicap the performance of your nascent inside sales team.

Obviously, there will be a concern that the inside salespeople and the field salespeople will—for this transitional period—end up stepping on each other's toes. This can be overcome by ensuring that your sales manager works closely with your campaign coordinator to ensure that inside sales approaches accounts without open opportunities—and with propositions that the field salespeople are not actively promoting. Of course, in the long run, this contention will disappear as all sales opportunities are owned internally.

As soon as you have inside salespeople, you want to push their activity level to thirty meaningful selling interactions a day. It's the job of your campaign coordinator to maintain opportunity queues sufficient to support this volume of activity. As inside sales activity levels increase, so will the volume of field visit requests generated by inside sales.

Step 6: Reconfigure Field Representatives

At some point in this process, you will need to convert your field salespeople from commissions to salary. Of course, you will need to advise them at the outset that this is inevitable—and assure them that they will not be disadvantaged by the transition.

It's okay to defer the change while you are working on customer service and on implementing inside sales, but as the percentage of activities scheduled from inside starts to increase, you will reach a point at which it no longer makes sense to treat field salespeople as autonomous agents. At that point, you must convert them to salary—either one at a time or all at once. If you don't, you will end up with conflict between field and inside salespeople. And this conflict will compromise both your new model and customer service quality.

Interestingly, most of our silent revolutionaries elect to tear off the bandage and make the change at the beginning of the transition—right after selling the new direction.

As the mix of field salespeople's activities starts to skew toward those activities that are planned from inside, you'll reach another tipping point. At some point, it will become clear to all parties that the field salespeople are more productive when they are responding to field visit requests generated from the inside sales team than they are when they originate and manage opportunities themselves. This is when you should transfer all opportunities to your inside sales team and allow the field salespeople to become dedicated field specialists. Of course, this change will result in a marked increase in the field specialists' available capacity—allowing you to continue to scale your inside sales team without adding field personnel.

One question I always get at this point in the discussion is: *What about those customers who demand (or who genuinely require) regular drop-ins from field representatives?* Interestingly, this new model does not preclude this kind of visit. If necessary, field specialists can program regular repeat visits in their calendars—or, if you have a field scheduler, your scheduler can plan these visits for them.

If you think about it, the inside-out model makes it easier to perform these visits, because the field personnel have so much more time available for face-to-face meetings. The big difference, however, is that in the inside-out model it will be abundantly clear if these *milk-run* visits are not an effective use of field specialists' time.

Once that has been determined, you can then focus on changing the nature of the relationship you have with those customers so that regular drop-ins are not required. A favorite tactic of our silent revolutionaries is to convert those customers who purchase regularly into some kind of vendor-managed inventory (VMI) arrangement.

Step 7: Build the Business-Development Function

This last point raises an interesting question of who should be responsible for upselling casual customers to a more strategic relationship. To set the scene, let's first explore the VMI proposition.

VMI is a relationship between a vendor and a customer in which the vendor owns and manages the customer's inventory—and bills them only at the point of consumption.

This is a powerful proposition for both the vendor and the customer. The customer benefits because they convert the inventory that currently sits on their balance sheet into cash and because they get better availability from a smaller inventory footprint. The vendor benefits because VMI creates a large switching cost for customers and because it protects the vendor's margins. If the vendor has a lot of VMI customers, this arrangement actually reduces the total volume of inventory the vendor has to hold to provide customers the same level of availability.

In case you're wondering, VMI works so well because the vendor has the ability to pool both customer data and demand. They also have total control over the customer's inventory levels, replenishment frequencies, and batch sizes.

The big problem with VMI is that typical field salespeople find it very hard to sell. It's not that it isn't an appealing proposition—it obviously is. The issue is that the VMI discussion requires that the salesperson and the customer have a relationship that's fundamentally different from the typical *what can I sell you today?* relationship. And even if the vendor is willing to elevate the relationship, the customer may not be.

If you have enough occasions to present your customers with a business proposition (as opposed to a transactional proposition) to warrant one or more dedicated business-development managers, it's time now to build a business-development function.

As we've discussed, this function will consist of pairs of BDMs and BDCs, along with project leaders if you're operating in an engineer-to-order environment.

When it comes down to it, this function is very easy to build, for two simple reasons: A true BDM (or *enterprise salesperson*, as they're often called) will just love the environment you are proposing for them. The idea of a dedicated executive assistant; no prospecting, customer service, or project management responsibilities; and a high volume of meaningful face-to-face meetings is so appealing that the right person will walk over broken glass to operate in this environment. And if you have already built a high-volume inside sales team, you will find that you are already surfacing a steady stream of business-development opportunities. For example, if you'd like to generate VMI opportunities, you can have your campaign coordinator and inside sales team organize (and populate) webinars or—better still—lunch-and-learn events.

❋ ❋ ❋ ❋

You now have a plan—or at least the skeleton of a plan. Let's push forward then, and see whether we can't put some meat on them bones!

Chapter 9
HOW TO CONVERT
OPPORTUNITIES INTO SALES

The next two chapters deal with opportunities: how to originate them and how to prosecute them. But as you'll notice from this chapter's title, we're not navigating this big subject in what would appear to be the logical order.

There are two (very) important reasons for which we'll be talking about prosecuting opportunities before we talk about originating them: Assuming that your business exists right now, the first set of opportunities you'll encounter are those that already exist—meaning that the content of this chapter is immediately applicable. Counter to popular opinion, there is typically—but not always—more upside in improving the management of your existing opportunity flow than there is in investing the same effort in the generation of new opportunities.

In this chapter, we'll define what we mean by *opportunity*, and then we'll figure out how to convert opportunities into sales.

WHAT IS A SALES OPPORTUNITY?

The definition of *sales opportunity* would appear to be self-evident: It's an opportunity to sell something. This definition, however, is a little imprecise. In practice, the term *sales opportunity* can mean two things, depending on the context: a potential deal that a salesperson is working on or a potential customer that's worthy of a salesperson's attention.

Obviously, there's potential for a gap between these two definitions; salespeople tend to use the first definition, and marketing people use the second. Marketing folks and salespeople will frequently disagree on whether a salesperson should be working a given opportunity.

For this reason, salespeople frequently use the term *qualified opportunity* to distinguish between the opportunities that marketing thinks they should be working on and those that they believe are worthy of their limited attention. Predictably, this results in endless—and not particularly productive—debates about whether opportunities are, in fact, opportunities!

A better approach is to settle on the first definition and then make marketing (your campaign coordinator) responsible for replenishing the opportunity queue as a salesperson's activity causes it to deplete. By establishing a *pull* relationship between sales and marketing, you have forced the two functions to work together.

So, an opportunity is a potential deal that a salesperson is working on or a potential deal that has been queued for a salesperson to work on within the current period. Now, if you think about it, the *potential deal* bit is redundant. In the inside-out model, salespeople don't work on anything else. Practically, then, sales opportunities are the raw material that salespeople work on.

When we come to consider technology, that practical definition is meaningful because it informs us that all—as in 100 percent—of the work that a salesperson (or a business-development coordinator) does should be done within the opportunity module in the customer relationship management application (CRM).

LET'S BE DONE WITH QUALIFICATION

A benefit of our definition is that we've done away with the requirement for *qualification*. In the inside-out model, a potential deal is either in the salesperson's opportunity queue or it isn't.

Sadly, the notion of qualification is so entrenched in sales environments that it doesn't simply fade away with the clarification of definitions. The thing is, in sales environments, it's widely believed that qualification is a necessary and value-adding activity. Nothing, however, could be further from the truth.

Let's consider qualification, as it's typically practiced.

Lenny, the CEO of a mobile-application-development firm, returns from a business-leaders' mixer with a handful of business cards. Each business card has been given to him by a senior executive from a midsize organization. Excited, he hands the twenty business cards to David, one of his salespeople, who agrees to follow them up.

Two weeks pass and Lenny has received no feedback, so he buttonholes David at the local cafeteria. "What's happened with those twenty opportunities I gave you?" he asks.

"Well," David explains, "only two of them are qualified . . . but don't worry, I'm still working on them."

Lenny is incredulous: "What do you mean, only two of them are qualified? All of those people are senior executives of decent-size businesses—and *all* decent-size businesses have cause to at least consider web applications."

David shrugs and returns to his lunch.

We can only make sense of David's position if we consider the environment in which he operates (the traditional model). Because of the multitude of competing demands for David's time, David has no choice but to prioritize. And because many of these demands are urgent (e.g., helping production interpret customer requests, solving customer service problems), David has very little capacity remaining to invest in speculative business-development activities.

When Lenny handed him the twenty business cards, David recognized that he simply didn't have time to prosecute twenty opportunities concurrently. His solution was to make a quick call to each contact to determine how interested they were in a mobile application (to determine if they were qualified). Not surprisingly, he discovered that only two of the twenty had any concrete interest; none of the others had even made a budgetary allocation!

Qualification is not selling; it's actually the opposite—the avoidance of selling. Of course, the core problem here is the design of the traditional sales environment. However, when we reengineer that environment, we cannot simply assume that all the practices that made sense in the old environment will simply disappear in the new one. Some won't, which means that they need to be actively eliminated.

Qualification is a particularly insidious—and remarkably persistent—practice. You will need to hunt it down and drive a stake through its ugly heart whenever it makes an appearance. If a salesperson has an unutilized unit of capacity and there's a potential deal in the queue, that salesperson should be selling, not qualifying.

A Standard Workflow

Now that we agree on what sales opportunities are, we can discuss how to prosecute them—how to convert a percentage of them into sales. For each opportunity type (sales objective), we need a standard workflow. A workflow is the sequence of steps that need to be performed in order to convert a potential customer into an actual one.

The most important steps tend to involve asking the prospect for an intermediate commitment of some kind (e.g., a web conference to present a proposal), and that exposes a central truth: We convince the prospect to make big commitments (purchases) by encouraging them to make a sequence of smaller commitments.

One Workflow

You should have only one workflow for each product or service. In fact, similar products should share the same workflow. If you receive opportunities from multiple promotional campaigns, those campaigns should all be designed to feed into the same workflow.

Standardization means that the path each opportunity follows through your organization is essentially the same as the path followed by the opportunity before it. There is certainly no reason for variation between salespeople, and even where customers are concerned, it is usually preferable to adopt a standard workflow, for two reasons: First, in a mature market, competitive pressures will cause your customers to structure their businesses similarly and to adopt similar procurement procedures; and second, in an immature market, customers will not have developed fixed procurement procedures—meaning that your salespeople have the opportunity to convince them to purchase via whatever sequence of steps you believe is optimal for both parties.

The best way to understand the opportunity-management workflow is to build or map one. To make this exercise challenging, we'll map a business-development workflow (as opposed to a simpler inside sales one). That means that this workflow would make sense in an environment such as that of James Sanders Group, in chapter 1.

Step 1: Assemble the Building Blocks

We've already discussed, at length, the resourcing component of business development. We know that where opportunity management is concerned, you have the following resource pool: a business-development coordinator, a business-development manager, and a project leader.

Let's now consider the activities—steps—that will be required to convert opportunities into sales. We can start by grouping them by general activity type: face-to-face appointments of various types (e.g., workshops, demonstrations); conference calls (voice and video); solution design, estimating, and quoting; scheduling activities (e.g., via phone, email); and various debriefing conversations between different parties, particularly between the salesperson and the business-development coordinator.

To enable the collection of meaningful management information, we need to identify milestones—stages—too. The ideal milestones are those locations in the workflow at which your customer has just agreed to proceed to the next meaningful activity, such as when the customer has scheduled an initial appointment, scheduled a proposal-review meeting (obviously, agreeing to a proposal-review meeting is more meaningful than simply agreeing to receive a proposal), scheduled a management workshop, or scheduled a contract-review meeting.

Now that we have all the components, it's time to assemble the first draft of your standard workflow. I say *first draft* because this initial diagram will almost certainly be redrawn multiple times before it's deemed fit for purpose!

For this, you'll need either a sheet of graph paper and a pencil or, better still, a charting program (my preference is Microsoft Visio[11]).

Step 2: Let's Go Swimming

Start by drawing a set of *swim lanes* (so named because collectively they resemble a swimming pool). It's standard practice to delineate resources on the horizontal and stages on the vertical (see figure 31). You can then name the workflow and each of the resources.

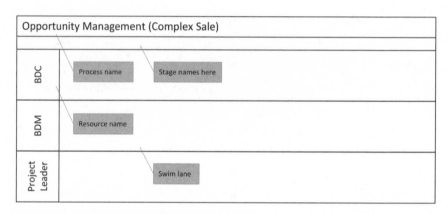

Figure 31. Delineate resources with swimlanes.

Step 3: A Simple, Linear Flow

You can now start to add entities and connectors. My recommendation is that you force yourself to map your entire workflow using only two entities: states and activities. States are inputs to—and outputs from—activities. This restraint will prevent you from mapping the workflow at too granular a level.

In case you're wondering, the ideal level of granularity is the one at which most activities are essential and all pairs of activities are noncommutative (i.e., their sequence can't be reversed—think of how washing and then drying clothes generates a different outcome from the alternate sequence).

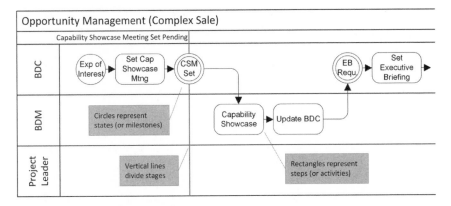

Figure 32. Example workflow, step 1.

If we examine the first few steps in this workflow (figure 32), we can make some interesting observations. In this instance, we're assuming the opportunity is triggered by an inbound inquiry, rather than an outbound campaign. The meetings have names—as opposed to being described by their location in the sequence (e.g., first meeting, second meeting). This is because it's the content of the meeting that's of primary importance. For example, a second meeting might be a repeat of the first meeting, or it may be a materially different event. The meeting name communicates the purpose of the meeting (and sometimes its intended outcome) to all parties. We map a single path with no loop-backs and no trivial activities (e.g., *update the CRM*). We do map the points at which the salesperson debriefs their business-development coordinator, because these activities are critical and should be tracked. The stage names reference the outcome of that subset of the process and conclude with the word *pending*. This focuses the team members on the concrete outcome rather than on the activities being performed. Finally, the business-development coordinator is the process owner. For this reason, most states (milestones) will appear in their swim lane.

Step 4: Complexity, Be Gone!

As we get deeper into this workflow and get more comfortable with the mapping method, we can turn our attention to the structure of the opportunity-management process. Specifically, we need to consider the differences between a workflow for a simple sale and one for a complex sale. Interestingly, there isn't much of a difference—at least there shouldn't be.

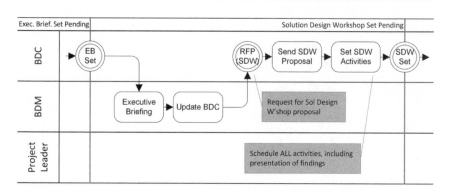

Figure 33. Example workflow, step 2.

Consider the continuation of our (complex-sale) workflow, shown in figure 33. To date, we've performed a couple of appointments: the first with our initial contact and the second with the team of decision makers. As a consequence, we've secured a request for a proposal. If this were a simple sale, we'd be proposing our ultimate offering at this point; however, because it's a complex sale, we're proposing an intermediate offering: a solution-design workshop.

You'll soon see that the solution-design workshop consists of a couple of appointments and terminates in the presentation of another proposal—in this case, for the final offering. However, if this sales opportunity were more complex still, the solution-design workshop might terminate in a proposal for a *pilot*, which—you guessed it—would be an engagement that leads to yet another proposal!

It should now be clear that a complex sale does not necessitate a complex opportunity-management process. Just as a centipede with 191 trunk segments is no more complex than a fly, which has only twelve, the complexity of an opportunity-management process does not increase as we accumulate multiple iterations of an inherently simple subprocess.

In summary, then, we prosecute a simple opportunity with a simple process (consisting of just a handful of activities). We prosecute a complex opportunity with the same simple process, repeated multiple times.

We've just stumbled across the secret of what's typically referred to as *major-account selling*. If you read books on this subject, you'll learn that the key to prosecuting complex deals is to get inside of—and attempt to manage—this complexity.

The reality is that *truly* complex deals tend to be too complex to manage (at least from the perspective of the salesperson). Rather than attempting the impossible, a better approach is to collaborate with your potential customer and find a way to *engineer the complexity out* of the engagement process. Of course, both you and your customers will benefit from the simplification of an otherwise unworkable workflow.

Step 5: Solution Design

We can now go ahead and complete the mapping of our representative opportunity-management process. And, with this done, I think you've earned yourself a cup of tea!

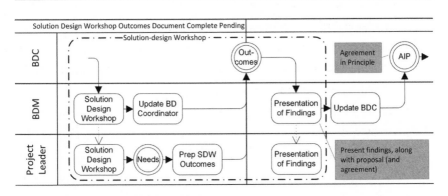

Figure 34. Example workflow, step 3.

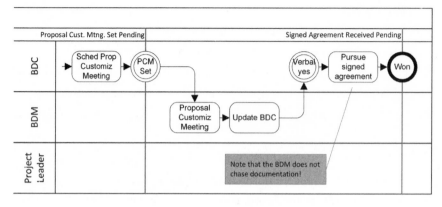

Figure 35. Example workflow, step 4.

THE SOLUTION-DESIGN WORKSHOP

A solution-design workshop is an invaluable addition to your opportunity-management workflow whenever you are selling a custom-engineered product or service. Such a workshop—often called a *feasibility study* or an *envisioning workshop*—provides the following benefits: It enables you to take control of your client's decision-making processes, which, absent your involvement, is often entirely unstructured and ineffective. It turns solution design into a collaborative process, which results in potential clients assuming ownership of the solution long before they are asked to purchase, and slashes the duration of the solution-design process. And it enables you to socialize the new direction with a larger number of stakeholders (on the client side) than would otherwise be possible.

The solution-design workshop should be facilitated either by a project leader or by a dedicated facilitator. In either case, your salesperson and nominated project leader must be present and must be actively involved in the workshop. You should design your workshop so that the greater proportion of the content that will ultimately populate your outcomes document (and the accompanying proposal) is actually generated during the workshop (excluding content that is standard to all documents, of course).

Ideally, the workshop should consist of a series of tightly choreographed exercises. You can conduct these exercises on a whiteboard, but my preference is to use a word processor and a charting application (in conjunction with a projector) as a virtual whiteboard.

The exercises are likely to include the following:

- a very brief introduction from the workshop sponsor (on the client side) and the project leader—including a summary of the scope of the workshop;
- the discovery of the sets of symptoms (i.e., undesirable effects) that have given cause to the workshop (I say sets of symptoms because you want to record the perspectives of multiple participants);
- reasoning from the undesirable effects to the root cause or causes of these effects;
- the determination of the direction of the solution;
- a high-level design of the solution (ideally using diagrams);
- the resolution of key lower-level design issues;
- a risk analysis (including a review of possible unintended consequences of the proposed solution);
- a high-level economic feasibility review (i.e., how will the organization justify the likely expenditure of money and other resources?).

After the workshop, the project leader should convert the outcomes into a formal presentation of findings document and review this document with the salesperson prior to the scheduled presentation of findings meeting. My preference is to create this document in PowerPoint or in a similar format. The format forces the project leader to reduce their findings to essentials— and it also allows the same document to be used as a presentation aid.

PROPOSALS, ESTIMATES, AND QUOTATIONS

Where proposals and other similar documentation are concerned, it's worth reviewing who should do what. We know already that we do not want the salesperson involved in the creation of any documentation, and we should also have a good idea about who will be responsible for the proposals for simple transactions (the customer service team) and complex transactions (the project leader). There are, however, some proposals that resist being squeezed into these two categories.

The Solution-Design Workshop Proposal

Take, for example, the solution-design workshop proposal: Who should prepare that? This proposal should be a stock-standard document—simply because all your solution-design workshops should use the same basic structure. Obviously, the duration of the event will vary from client to client—as will the name of the client! But all such variability can, and should, be accommodated with a simple automated Word document like the one shown in figure 36. Consequently, a solution-design workshop proposal can be generated by a BDC within seconds.

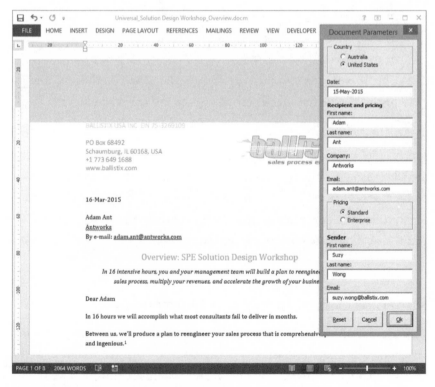

Figure 36. With some simple scripting an advanced user can automate the generation of standard documents using Microsoft Word, Google Docs, or other word processing applications.

Proposals for Complicated (but Not Complex) Products

We've already resolved that a complex sale is one in which a perfect hand-off between sales and production is impossible. This definition leaves room for situations in which the quote is still pretty complicated because of either the technical or the commercial requirements.

In these situations, you need to ensure that the salesperson captures all of the information required to generate the proposal in the sales meeting. In other words, the salesperson should be able to submit all the data required to generate the proposal to their business-development coordinator at the conclusion of the meeting. This might involve emailing a PowerPoint or Excel file or simply pressing *submit* within a custom mobile application.

Salespeople are likely to object that they need to customize the sales preamble at the start of the proposal and that this cannot be done in front of the customer.

This is simply not true.

The reality is that customers, if they have invested the time required to meet with a salesperson, would rather receive a proposal that accurately captures both the commercial and technical realities of their situation. Furthermore, in many cases, customers will intend to take the proposal and use it to influence others in the organization who aren't present in the meeting—meaning that they will value the salesmanship encapsulated in the document.

DEMONSTRATIONS

As is evidenced by the pitch doctors who sell nifty potato peelers in shopping centers, nothing sells like a good demonstration. Sometimes, however, the demonstration is a distraction from what you are trying to sell. Demonstrations can destroy much value in complex sales environments, particularly among technology companies. Here's a scenario.

Imagine that you're the financial controller of a business that does $100 million a year in sales, and you're considering purchasing a new enterprise resource planning (ERP) system. Ask yourself what you are really buying. Are you buying a piece of software, or are you buying a better approach to governance, to management decision making, and to operational performance that will (hopefully) be facilitated by a software application?

It's the latter, isn't it?

Now ask yourself this: If you stare long and hard at the software, is there any likelihood that the business outcomes you're looking for will suddenly appear? Of course not. The software is a distraction from what you're buying. A smart ERP vendor will not show it to you. Rather than demoing software, this vendor will talk to you about the assumptions, theories, and methodologies that are baked into their software. They'll understand that if they can sell the theoretical underpinnings of their software, you will lose interest in examining the application itself. They'll assume that if you're one of the very few software vendors who are capable of having a high-level discussion about the realities of business management, you've probably also figured out how to build software that works.

One of our silent revolutionaries—a particularly successful enterprise software producer—has discovered that it makes sense to postpone demonstrations as long as possible and then to finally show the software in the form of training sessions for users, with decision makers looking on.

Continuous Improvement

We're about to turn our attention to the generation of sales opportunities—a big and exciting subject! However, before we do, I must reiterate my exhortation that you first pay attention to the prosecution of your existing opportunity flow.

I hope this chapter has made it clear what a big subject opportunity management is and that it has provided you with numerous ideas for improvement. Please be sure to exploit all of these ideas before you shift your attention to promotion.

Chapter 10
HOW TO GENERATE SALES OPPORTUNITIES

If you're not in the fortunate situation in which promotion is easy, the odds are that it's very difficult. If you're in the latter category, this chapter will introduce you to the magnitude of the promotional challenge ahead and explain why moderate success is (fortunately) probably more than sufficient in the early stages of your transition to the inside-out model. It'll also walk you through the process of creating your first set of promotional campaigns.

Now, if it sounds like I'm trying to recalibrate your expectations at the start of this important chapter, you're absolutely right: I am! In my experience, most managers underappreciate the magnitude of the promotional challenge and, consequently, fail to make a sufficient commitment to it. Campaigns are launched with unrealistic expectations and then initial successes are overlooked. The end result is that promotion is regarded as a black art, and management places occasional bets on whatever happens to be the promotional flavor of the month, motivated more by a sense of obligation than by any real expectation of results.

This, of course, is a vicious cycle. If we're to break the cycle, we need to replace the sequence above with this one:

- Engineer a sales function that can operate quite comfortably with little more than your existing *organic* opportunity flow.
- Run small promotional experiments and evaluate all outcomes objectively.
- Iterate rapidly, but be prepared for the development of an effective promotional function to take many months (if not years).

- Finally, steel yourself for the journey by reminding yourself, regularly, that a sales function without a scalable source of opportunities is not much of a sales function, just as a business without a scalable source of sales is not much of a business.

WHY PROMOTION IS EITHER EASY OR REALLY, REALLY DIFFICULT

It's instructive to examine those rare businesses that find promotion easy. I think it's fair to say that these organizations tend to find themselves in this enviable position for one of two reasons: Either they have invented a breakthrough product—the proverbial *better mousetrap*—and the world genuinely is beating a path to their door, or they have invented a space in the mind of the market and, within that space, they are regarded as the thought leaders.

It's easy to see that promotion will be easy if you are a product or thought leader; think of Apple after the launch of their game-changing iPhone or HubSpot and their inbound marketing[12] method. However, if you're not in one of these categories, it's also easy to see why promotion is difficult. Absent a breakthrough product or a position of thought leadership, you may lack a compelling message, an attentive audience, or both. That's not to say that you can't emulate the promotional activities of Apple and HubSpot. You can; you just can't expect those activities to yield the same results.

The thing is, if you have established a leadership position in your market, your promotional activities need only communicate that good news. However, if you lack this leadership, your promotional activities *are* the news. Consequently, they will be less effective and more likely to suffer from rapidly diminishing returns.

A BITTER PILL

In case you're wondering, there's a reason management tends to under-appreciate the magnitude of the promotional challenge. Under the old model, the responsibility for the origination of sales opportunities rests with salespeople. Management may recognize some responsibility for tilling the soil via marketing activities, but the general assumption is that promotion (or *prospecting*, as salespeople like to call it) is just part of selling. In the inside-out model, this responsibility is taken away from salespeople and transferred inside, leaving management no choice but to confront the promotional challenge head on.

Now, here's a bitter pill. If you find yourself in a position in which promotion is really difficult, it's likely that you will need to look outside your marketing department for a long-term solution to this problem. Without a product- or thought-leadership position, your promotional activities are severely handicapped, meaning that you will struggle to find campaigns that generate better than marginal returns.

What I'm suggesting, then—lest there be any confusion—is that, in the long run, if you are not currently either a product or a thought leader, it's easier to become one than it is to attempt to compensate with acts of promotional gallantry.

Of course, the development of either product or thought leadership is outside the mandate of this book. Both require innovation, and this innovation must be driven from the very top of the organization. And both require initiatives that cross many divisional boundaries, involving engineering, sales, production, and finance.

WHY MODERATE SUCCESS IS MORE THAN SUFFICIENT

Fortunately, there is good news. If your organization is typical, it will be possible for you to make the transition to the inside-out model, and to generate a meaningful increase in sales performance with only minimal promotional effort.

This is because the old model is so terribly inefficient! Specifically, it tends to result in both accounts and opportunities being seriously underexploited. Accounts are underexploited because salespeople are too busy with customer service (including the processing of repeat transactions) to dedicate much attention to business development, and opportunities are underexploited because salespeople insist on engaging only with qualified opportunities.

For this reason, it's likely that you will be able to generate all the opportunities you need to at least double your current volume of sales activities (field meaningful selling interactions) simply by pitching new service lines to existing accounts (rather than simply processing repeat transactions) and engaging with all existing accounts more frequently—particularly those that are not already heavy users of your services—and by eliminating qualification and engaging with everyone who is a genuine prospect (capacity permitting).

It's important that you remember that your initial objective is only to increase your volume of sales activity by between two and five times (depending on your mix of inside to outside activity). And as we discussed in chapter 7, it's critical that you ensure that your sales team is no larger than is required to service this volume of opportunities.

So, if you have sized your sales team correctly and if you fully exploit both existing accounts and your existing opportunity flow, you should have no need for additional promotion (over and above what you are doing now)—at least on paper!

In reality, however, it's likely that you will still be tempted to engage in some additional promotional activities, perhaps to compensate for quieter periods or to raise your quality of opportunities. And that's okay. Because, in these scenarios, your requirement for opportunities is low, you should be able to make do with short-term, tactical campaigns, deferring the requirement to tackle some of the bigger promotional challenges.

GETTING PREPARED

As you may have noticed, I'm using the word *promotion* to refer to the origination of sales opportunities. You know from the previous chapter that a *sales opportunity* is a potential deal that a salesperson is working on.

Therefore, *promotion* is the process of identifying prospects and allocating them to salespeople.

A *prospect* is either an individual or an organization that has a nonzero likelihood of purchasing within a reasonable time horizon. As is illustrated in figure 37, a prospect can be either an existing customer (who has the potential to buy more) or a potential customer.

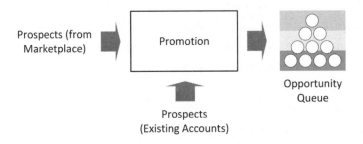

Figure 37. The purpose of promotion is to populate (and replenish) salespeople's opportunity queues.

Unlike salespeople, marketing communicates with prospects in batches, or cohorts. We use the word *campaign* to refer to both the communication and the cohort of prospects who are being communicated with.

You may have noticed that the only concept here that implies a value judgment is *prospect*. A *sales opportunity* is simply the raw material that a salesperson works on. *Promotion* is simply the process of finding and queuing that raw material. And a *campaign* is simply a cohort of prospects (and the communication we have with that cohort).

The simplification (or sanitization) of these concepts makes communication easier and, to a great extent, eliminates the kind of semantic debates you frequently hear in sales environments.

Now, that's not to say that quality is not important. Obviously, if we're going to give salespeople projects to work on, we should push the best to the very front of the queue. The point is that we need to be able to discuss the basic structure of the sales function using value-neutral terms.

Who Is Responsible for Promotion?

As you know, most of our silent revolutionaries have a person called a *campaign coordinator*, who is technically a member of the marketing team but who is on permanent loan to sales.

This campaign coordinator is responsible for running the sets of (often) daily campaigns required to maintain salespeople's opportunity queues at their optimal sizes. It makes a lot of sense for this person to live in the sales department because they must adopt the sales department's cadence, which is much faster than that of the marketing department, and because it's critical that they have a firsthand appreciation of how campaigns are being received by the marketplace.

The campaign coordinator can either draw on the marketing department for promotional collateral or commission collateral from third parties (marketing departments are often better at general marketing communications than they are at campaign-related collateral).

Campaign Ingredients

All promotional campaigns have three fundamental ingredients:

1. an offer, the basic proposition the campaign presents;
2. an audience, the set of individuals to which the campaign is targeted; and
3. communication, how the offer communicated—the creative execution.

These ingredients are listed in order of significance. Item 1 has roughly an order of magnitude more impact on the effectiveness of the campaign than item 2, and item 2 is an order of magnitude more important than item 3.

To illustrate the relative significance of these ingredients, let's consider a simple scenario. We'll assume that you have a nice car—a late-model BMW M3, perhaps—and that you are determined to dispose of this car in a hurry. Assume that you park your car on a busy street and paint the following in white paint on the rear window:

FOR SALE: BMW M3
$15,000

There should be no question that this campaign will quickly draw a crowd. At best, you'll sell your car quickly. At worst, you'll cause a traffic jam and get arrested for causing a public nuisance.

The value of this scenario is that it makes the relative importance of the promotional ingredients obvious. It's clear that the size of the traffic jam you create will primarily be a function of the desirability of the car in conjunction with the price you paint on the rear window—the *offer*, in other words.

Audience is important, but not nearly as important as the offer. If you really are selling your late-model M3 for $15,000, you can park your car on a quiet street in the middle of the night and word will still get out. And it's clear that this campaign is not super sensitive to creative execution. You can communicate your message effectively with five words and one critical number. In fact, I suspect the market will even forgive you a spelling mistake or two!

A failure to appreciate the relative importance of the offer is at the heart of many promotional problems. It's certainly convenient for managers to assume that their product is inherently desirable and to focus, instead, on the fun stuff—pretty pictures, snappy prose, and clever videos.

A more prudent approach is to consider creative execution only after you have developed a truly compelling offer, and an offer can be considered compelling only after it has demonstrated its ability to pull a crowd in real-world tests. Until such an offer has been developed, it is safer to ignore the other promotional ingredients altogether. More correctly, you should confirm both that your offer is clearly communicated and that your campaign is being exposed to individuals who match the profile of existing customers. If you can tick both these boxes, you are free to focus exclusively on the offer.

Campaign Structure

A novice could be excused for presuming that a promotional campaign is a single event. This, however, is often not the case. Campaigns are similar to opportunities in that they often consist of a series of activities, or steps. If we imagine that we are attempting to generate opportunities for the sale of enterprise software, a single campaign might consist of the following steps: (a) a pay-per-click advertisement, encouraging viewers to view a video detailing enterprise software horror stories, which directs the viewers to (b) a landing (or squeeze) page, containing the video and a pitch for the visitors to request a software buyers' guide, the dispatch of which will be followed by (c) an email campaign directed to readers of the buyers' guide, inviting them to attend a webinar, and then, finally, the webinar itself, designed to upsell to a business-process-modeling workshop. We'll assume that those who register for the workshop are classified as *opportunities* and handed off to the salespeople or business-development coordinators.

Campaigns have multiple steps for the same reason opportunities do—namely, it is often unrealistic (or uneconomic) to pitch the ultimate objective at the first point of contact with the market.

A Testing-Based Framework

Smart marketers know their limitations.

It's simply not possible to *design* a successful campaign; you need to *evolve* one through a framework of trial and error. And at the heart of this process, we have the AB test.

In an AB test, you simply test two (or more) variations of the campaign to determine which performs better. The real magic is not the test itself, but rather the iterative framework that encapsulates the test:

1. Assume your current campaign (*the control*) is suboptimal (always!).
2. Create a variation of the control campaign.
3. Test the variation against the control (ensuring that the test is statistically valid).
4. Establish the winning variant as the new control, then repeat from step 1.

A marketing genius is someone who accepts that they will never truly understand how the market thinks but who is committed to an ongoing process of testing and refinement.

The first question is what to test, and we know the answer to that question already. Because the offer has disproportionate influence on the performance of a campaign, we should test the offer first—and frequently. The next thing to test is the audience. (In practice, this means running your campaign in different mediums.) The third thing to test is creative execution (communication).

The second question is how to test. The theory is simple. To test, you run two versions of the one campaign in parallel and determine which produces the better return on promotional spending. As well as testing discrete campaign elements, you can—and should—test different campaign structures.

If you are running an online campaign, testing is likely to be easy. Most providers of online advertising allow you to create multiple versions of a campaign and then serve these versions randomly to site visitors. In addition, there are services that enable you to run AB tests on your landing pages and on various components of your website.

With the exception of email and direct mail campaigns, testing can require much greater effort offline. The problem is that traditional media (e.g., TV, newspapers, magazines) do not allow you to present two campaigns to a single audience at a single point in time. To compensate for this, you need to run multiple tests to compile meaningful data. For example, to test a newspaper advertisement, you will need to run two versions of the advertisement in different papers on day 1 and then repeat the exercise, switching the ad versions on day 2. This will allow you to control for the two different audiences and the two different days.

YOUR FIRST CAMPAIGNS

Okay. Time to take all that theory and figure out how to apply it in practice. Rather than talking about campaigns in the abstract, let's discuss actual campaigns you might run as you transition from the traditional to the inside-out model.

Table 3 includes a list of likely campaigns in the order you might run them.

Table 3. Likely campaigns.

Campaign name	Objective	Offer	Audience
Time for a coffee	Preapproach email: Schedule catch-up meetings between accounts and salespeople	Meeting (and coffee)	Existing accounts (primary contact)
Reconsider? An irresistible proposition	Preapproach email: Compel lost opportunities to reengage (book meeting)	Irresistible deal—with conditions	Late-stage opportunities that were recently lost
Webinar: A DIY guide	Generate opportunities from house list	Best-practices briefing (meeting)	Entire house list
E-book: Top 10 reasons	Use PPC and SEO to build house list	E-book with registration (first name and email)	Finance officers in midsized companies

Time for a Coffee

Your first campaign should be a very simple one. Your initial objective should be simply to get the entire sales machine moving. After all, with even the simplest campaign imaginable, there are still quite a few moving parts that must be coordinated: Of course, you need an offer, a target audience, and a creative (the email, in this case). You need to build a list and broadcast the email to that list. You need to generate one opportunity for each campaign recipient (ideally, in a single batch). And you need to transfer those opportunities to a business-development coordinator (or directly to an inside sales team).

In this case, we intend to have our business-development coordinators schedule visits only between salespeople and existing accounts. We have no real offer, because we can probably assume that your existing accounts are happy to meet with a salesperson.

Now, you'll probably hear the argument that no email is required to preempt such a simple call. That's true, but you should send one anyway. After all, you're putting your entire sales machine through its paces, and promotions are an essential part of this machine.

In addition, there are two more reasons it makes sense to institute a policy that *all* outbound opportunities originate with a preapproach campaign. (An *outbound* opportunity is one that you initiate, rather than one resulting from an inbound inquiry.) A preapproach email will reduce the amount of time your business-development coordinators need to spend on the telephone (the call becomes essentially a scheduling call), and preapproach campaigns force the integration of your campaign coordinator and the rest of sales and, consequently, result in more forethought and greater management visibility.

Your very first promotional campaign (an email) is likely to look something like the following:

> Subject: Time for a coffee
>
> Hey Bob
>
> Susan asked me to reach out to you and organize a time for you and her to have a coffee in the next week or so.
>
> She would like to share a couple of case studies from your industry and, in particular, seek your input on a concept our engineering team has under development.
>
> I'll give you a call shortly to see if we can get this coffee scheduled.
>
> Jennifer (assistant to Susan Fisher)

You'll probably notice a few interesting things about this email. First, even though it is the first interaction between Bob and Susan's new business-development coordinator, it doesn't highlight Jennifer's addition to the team; in our experience, this is simply not necessary. Second, even though this meeting has no formal objective (which is not normally the case), the email does define an agenda and infer an objective (get input on a concept under development). Finally, the email does not look like a promotional email; it contains no advertising speak, no pretty pictures,[13] and no *unsubscribe* link.

Logistics

Because this is the first promotional campaign you've run under this new regime, it's worth detailing the steps required to execute the campaign and to transfer opportunities to the business-development coordinators.

Your campaign coordinator should create and save a filter (or view) in your customer relationship management (CRM) application that contains a list of all contacts that are eligible for this campaign (in this case, all primary contacts associated with active accounts). They should then select a small subset of this list (enough to represent a few days' worth of work for a single business-development coordinator) and associate this cohort with a new campaign. They should then broadcast the email to that cohort and, immediately afterward, generate a sales opportunity for each email sent. The opportunity should be associated with the account to which the contact belongs—and not directly with the contact—and the opportunity owner should be the business-development coordinator. Your campaign coordinator should then monitor the size of the business-development coordinator's queue of open opportunities and trigger the next broadcast only when the queue falls below a predetermined threshold (this concept is discussed in detail in the next chapter).

Reconsider? An Irresistible Proposition

Now that you've got your machine working and your salespeople (and your accounts) accustomed to the idea of working with a business-development coordinator, you're ready to progress to a campaign that incorporates some salesmanship.

In this case, we'll reach out to those opportunities that said *no* to you recently and see whether we can get them to reconsider. This campaign is interesting because it provides us with an excuse to grapple with the concept of *discounting*.

First, however, it's worth noting that a simple campaign like this can be extremely effective. You'll likely discover that a small percentage of lost opportunities can be reactivated—and subsequently sold—if you are prepared to make a small concession (a better price or some other benefit with purchase). And this incremental sales lift can have an outsized impact on your profitability over time.

When Discounting Makes Sense

Now, discounting is a sensitive subject, because we've all been brainwashed by business authors into believing that discounting is always a destructive activity. Here are the dangers we've been warned about: Discounting reduces your profitability, and the revenue increase required to recover that lost profitability is the inverse of the discount; discounting trains customers to alter their behavior so that they can consistently purchase at lower prices; and discounting triggers a price war—leading to a race to the bottom.

These are all valid concerns; however, they don't tell the whole story. For example, if the campaign I'm proposing causes you to win a sale that you would otherwise have lost and if that transaction does not place an additional load on your current system constraint, it causes no reduction in profitability—in fact, the opposite is the case. In addition, if this offer is made only for genuine sales opportunities—as opposed to transactions—it's unlikely to have a meaningful impact on customer behavior. Remember, we're using the word *sale* to refer to new accounts or new lines for existing accounts.

As far as price wars are concerned, your discount (or benefit with purchase) should always have strings attached. In other words, I'm suggesting that you should never offer a discount without imposing a condition or two. If you ensure that your discounts always have strings attached, you should be able to prevent your competitors (and your customers) from converting a one-off offer into a general price reduction.

Here are some examples of the kind of conditions you should attach to discounts (or benefits with purchase):

- It should be valid only for first-time purchases of particular service lines.
- It should be valid only if delivery is between certain dates (to take advantage of a temporary hole in your production schedule).
- It should be valid only if the customer allows six weeks for delivery.

And here's an example of a possible preapproach campaign email.

> Subject: Reconsider a Solution Design Workshop? An irresistible proposition
>
> Hi Bob
>
> We were all disappointed when you elected not to proceed with our proposed Solution Design Workshop.
>
> However, I'm happy to report that we've been able to identify an opportunity for you to purchase this engagement at a considerable discount if you are prepared to schedule it for February 20 and 21.
>
> This date range is significant because it spans President's Day, and, for this reason, that period is proving difficult for us to schedule.
>
> The good news is that we will provide you a $2,000 discount on the proposed Solution Design Workshop if you are able to schedule it for (only) these dates. The bad news is that we've made this offer simultaneously to two other organizations, and we can only accommodate one workshop.
>
> I'll give you a call shortly to see if you'd like to take advantage of this opportunity.
>
> Jennifer (Assistant to Susan Fisher)

Webinar: A DIY Guide

This next campaign is more ambitious still. It consists of four steps:

1. Send an (email) invitation to the webinar.

2. Call a subset of prospects to encourage them to register.

3. Conduct the webinar and upsell to the best-practices briefing (sales meeting).

4. Call to schedule meetings.

The Invitation

The creation of the invitation is where 90 percent of the decisions for the campaign as a whole get made. In fact, it makes a lot of sense to create the invitation and then design the webinar content on the basis of the invitation, rather than the other way around. This maximizes the likelihood that you will end up with a compelling event.

Your webinar should be a do-it-yourself guide to solving a problem you're convinced is afflicting a significant percentage of your target customers. It should not be a sales presentation.

For example, if you are attempting to sell project-management services to local government, your webinar invitation might look something like this:

Subject: Webinar: Meticulous planning—the enemy of public works projects

Why meticulous planning is guaranteeing that your public works projects will run behind schedule

Brenda

This free webinar shows how Northern Rivers was able to deliver 94% of works projects on time last year.

Conventional wisdom is wrong

Beyond a critical level of detail, more granular planning will guarantee that your projects run late. What's more, your contractors know this and are conspiring to use your meticulous plans against you!

This webinar will introduce you to a radically different approach to project management and share the recent journey—and impressive results—of Northern Rivers County.

Plan big, execute small

In 45 action-packed minutes, you'll learn . . .

Registration Calls

Once you have the invitation, you can go ahead and broadcast it to your list. Actually, what you should do is create a couple of variations on the invitation, send each to small subsets of your list, and then broadcast the best-performing one to the balance of the list.

It's now worth selecting another subset of your list and performing follow-up calls to see whether you can secure registrations. This activity can be performed either by your inside sales team (if you have one) or by temporary labor.

If you have a small list, these calls may be necessary to populate your webinar. Either way, it's worth running the test so that you can calculate the impact of follow-up calls.

Webinar

As soon as you have sent the invitations, you need to create the webinar itself. Specifically, you need to create an autoresponder sequence—a series of reminders—for registrants and a slide deck for the presenter.

The starting point for the latter is the offer. At this particular step in the campaign, you're upselling to a best-practices briefing (a meeting). First, create the slide for this briefing. Be sure to spell out a detailed agenda for the briefing to make it clear that this is not a thinly veiled sales presentation (see figure 38).

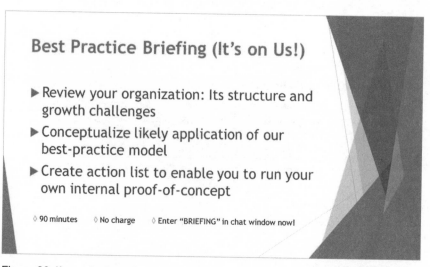

Figure 38. If you don't spell-out the value to be delivered in your post-webinar meeting, attendees will assume that it'll be nothing but a sales pitch

The briefing slide should be inserted in the middle (and at the end) of the presentation. The primary pitch for the briefing should be in the middle of the event, *not* at the end. This is because people will start checking out of your webinar the instant they sense that the primary content is drawing to a close.

What you leave out of your webinar is probably more important than what you put in. Be sure *not* to include an introduction to your organization and the presenter. These can be included in the pre-event materials—and, anyway, people are more than capable of inferring your professionalism from the quality of the event. Do not include instructions on how to use the webinar facility; you can include a link to these in your autoresponder sequence. Leave out small talk and meaningless verbiage (e.g., "in this fast-paced business environment . . . ").

Your webinar should start with a promise (how the attendee will benefit) and proceed directly to the meat and potatoes. The key to making the content compelling is to ensure that you teach the attendees something that they genuinely do not know and that you are presenting this knowledge in plain English, so that they can—at least, in theory—take it and apply it that very day.

Remember, you gain nothing by holding back knowledge. Your methods and practices are more valuable when you give them away than they are when you try to sell them.[14] By giving them away, you demonstrate your mastery of the subject matter and convince the prospects that they are better served leaving the execution to an expert.

As was mentioned earlier, you should pitch your offer—in this case, a best-practices briefing—in the middle of the event, right before some particularly juicy content. After mentioning the exciting content that follows, you should click to a slide that describes the briefing in detail (i.e., that presents the agenda for the meeting). You should then ask the attendees to express interest, either by responding to a poll or by entering the word *briefing* in the chat window.

Call to Schedule Meeting

In most cases, it makes sense to generate opportunities for your business-development coordinators in two batches: those attendees who expressed interest in a briefing (these can be scheduled right away), and everyone else (these can be called and offered one anyway!).

E-book: Top Ten Reasons

I hope you've noticed that all the campaigns thus far have been directed at your existing house list (accounts and prospects). It's critical that you exploit the value in your existing list before you invest money in the acquisition of new prospects in the *cold* market.

However, at some point you'll be keen to take the next step and tackle the wider marketplace. My suggestion is that you initially decouple your cold promotional activities from sales. In other words, focus on campaigns to build your house list rather than to directly generate opportunities. I recommend this because your first experiments with cold campaigns are likely to yield highly variable results. The last thing you should do at this point is inject this uncertainty into the front end of your sales process.

Of course, as you build your house list, new prospects can be converted into opportunities either via simple two-step (email then phone) campaigns or, better still, via webinars (or traditional events).

Now you build your house list by compelling your prospects to provide you with their contact information. You should attempt to gather only the information that you intend to use right away. In other words, if you intend to communicate with new prospects by email, you should ask them only for their first name and email address. An attempt to gather any more information will significantly reduce your return on promotional expenditure.

In order to get prospects to provide their contact information, you must first attract their attention and must then provide them with some kind incentive (such as an offer) to take a risk on you. The prospects are well aware that the cost of divulging their contact information is an increase in their volume of inbound email. The best way to do this is to give away something of significant value absolutely free of charge! Offers that fit this bill include product samples and packaged information (e.g., books, videos). The advantage of the latter is that they can be fulfilled electronically—meaning there is no fulfillment cost.

In this campaign, we plan to give away an e-book, which belongs in the second category. It's important, however, not to underestimate the potential of the first category.

Claude Hopkins is regarded by many to be the father of modern advertising. He also popularized the practice of sampling. In his classic 1923 book, *Scientific Advertising* (still as relevant today as it was ninety years ago!), he waxed lyrical about the benefits of samples. Two of the benefits he noted back then are that the offer of a sample can significantly increase the readership of your advertisement, and that prospects, when requesting a (physical) sample, will provide you with their physical addresses and, in almost every case, their phone numbers.[15]

One of our silent revolutionaries—a manufacturer of flexible heaters—offers its prospects a coffee warmer in kit form. Their prospects assemble it, and, more often than not, give it pride of place on their office desks!

E-book Content

Your e-book can be a whitepaper, a report, or an extract from a traditional book, and it can be delivered in PDF, Kindle, or any one of a number of other digital formats. The one thing it *can't* be is a document that resembles the sort of brochureware that's typically churned out by marketing departments and PR firms. If it isn't the kind of document that *you* would be prepared to pay for, don't even think about using it as the offer for this campaign.

One way to discipline yourself to write interesting copy is to start with the least self-serving (working) title you can possibly imagine. For example, if you are ultimately selling accounting software, you might commence with the following: *The Top Ten Reasons the Best Accounting Package is the One You Already Own.*

You'll almost certainly find that fifteen pages of copy begging readers not to waste money on unnecessary software will do a better job of selling your application than a hundred pages of standard marketing prose—assuming, of course, that your product services a legitimate need!

Advertising

Now that you have your e-book, the next step is to give it away. This requires two creative elements: an advertisement (to grab people's attention) and a landing page (to capture visitors' contact details).

There are numerous places you can run advertisements—everywhere from your local cinema (which is not a great idea) to *The New York Times* (which can be a great idea, once you know for sure you have a winning campaign on your hands).

If you trust me (and I'm sure you do by now), you'll avoid cinemas, national newspapers, billboards, and skywriting and go directly to online advertising—or, more specifically, to pay-per-click (PPC) advertising.

There's a bunch of reasons it makes sense to start here:

- Online is where your potential customers are.
- You can start with a very small budget—realistically, as little as $500.
- AB testing is easy, and you can collect meaningful results within hours.
- It's easier online than it is in any other medium to identify the source of sales opportunities.

For all these reasons, PPC is the very best environment to fine-tune your offer. Even if it ultimately makes sense to advertise in local papers or on television (which it may well), you should still keep returning to the Internet to test alternate approaches.

As I write this, Google is the best-known source of PPC advertising but not necessarily the most economic. My favored source of PPC advertising for business customers is LinkedIn, followed by Facebook. However, because things change fast online, you should not rely on this book for placement advice.

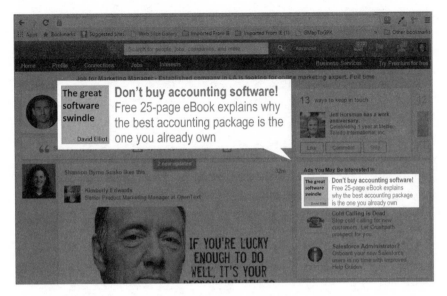

Figure 39. A mockup of what your PPC advertisement might look like (superimposed on a LinkedIn page for context).

Your PPC advertisement should point to a landing (or squeeze) page. The landing page will be a long and detailed advertisement for the book. Ideally, it will contain extracts from the book, testimonials from past readers, and even a video encouraging the visitor to provide their details now—so that they can receive your e-book in their inbox—within seconds, of course! And above all, the landing page will also contain the form that visitors will use to request the e-book.

Slow and Steady

In describing your first promotional steps, I've deliberately targeted campaigns that are relevant to a range of organizations and that are relatively simple.

Nonetheless, it should be clear that even these four simple campaigns involve quite a bit of work—particularly for organizations that have left the generation of sales opportunities up to their salespeople.

As I've stressed, a slow-and-steady approach to promotion is prudent. The process of trial and error required to arrive at effective offers and overall campaigns is time consuming, but when you factor in that truly effective promotions will likely require changes to the fabric of the larger organization, an overzealous approach can do enormous damage to your sales-improvement initiative.

COLD CALLING IS DEAD

On the subject of damaging your sales-improvement initiative, it would be remiss of me to end this chapter without discussing cold calling as a means of originating sales opportunities. There is a small number of (quite vocal) salespeople and sales managers who continue to champion the cause of cold calling. In addition, there are telemarketing bureaus that add voices to the choir.

The harsh reality, however, is that cold calling is dead, and it's been dead for years!

If you examine those salespeople who trumpet the effectiveness of cold calling, you'll discover that they spend an enormous amount of time on the phone to generate very few opportunities. You'll also discover that their prospecting work is so unpleasant that few—if any—of their colleagues are prepared to replicate it.

If you talk to those salespeople who receive sales opportunities that have been originated by cold calling, they'll tell you that these are their lowest-quality opportunities. On many occasions, the prospects are hostile, because they feel that they have been pestered and strong-armed into accepting appointments. If you examine the books of outbound telemarketing bureaus, you'll find that their average customer tenure is shockingly low—as low, in fact, as their internal staff turnover is high.

The problem with cold calling is that it simply doesn't make sense for your customers. You can take in a number of advertisements along with your primary search results on Google, for example, with negligible incremental effort. Imagine, however, that rather than placing those ads with your search provider, all those vendors were to ring you at work, one after another?

Of course, this used to happen. For this reason, most organizations have hidden their executives behind executive assistants and phone systems that force callers to announce themselves by recording a short message.

It may be true that good old Stan can cold call to generate all his sales opportunities. But if you can't recruit other Stans—and if no one else on the sales force is able or willing to replicate Stan's practices—you must face reality. Cold calling is dead.

❈ ❈ ❈ ❈

You now know how to generate and manage sales opportunities—the lifeblood of your reengineered sales function. Like the circulatory system, opportunity flow is necessary but not sufficient. There are other processes required to keep the organism alive and healthy. The last two chapters tackle two of them: technology and management.

Chapter 11
TECHNOLOGY: WHY CRM SUCKS!

Most managers are excited by technology. Technology enables us to get more done, faster. And technology is practical, concrete. It's not about ideas; it's about *execution*.

This is certainly true in sales environments. It's almost impossible to propose any initiative without prompting the question: *Is there software for that?*

In sales environments, the answer to that question is *yes*. There is always software for that. In fact, there are many thousands of software applications promising to automate every step in the sales lifecycle, from the generation of sales opportunities through the provision of management information.

BROKEN PROMISES

The dirty secret of sales environments is that, with few exceptions, this technology has done nothing to improve productivity. Nothing!

After a generation of investment in sales and marketing automation technologies, sales environments look and operate essentially the same as they did twenty years ago. There is little credible evidence that the tens—or, more commonly, hundreds—of thousands of dollars that a typical firm has spent on sales technology has caused a rise in revenues, a reduction in costs, or even an improvement in customer service quality.[16]

This chapter addresses three critically important questions:

1. Why is technology failing to produce the productivity improvements in sales that it has in other parts of the organization?
2. What role should technology play in the design and operation of the sales function?
3. What are the practical technology requirements of an organization transitioning to the inside-out model?

At the end of the chapter, we'll tackle another more fundamental technology issue. We'll explore who in the organization should accept which technology responsibilities and, more critically, which responsibilities should never be outsourced.

THE SALES SOFTWARE SYSTEM

If the multitude of sales-related software applications were a planetary system, the sun around which all other planets orbit would be the customer relationship management application (CRM). A CRM is designed to automate the numerous workflows that exist in and around the sales environment and to store the data that's generated as a result of those workflows. These workflows include the generation of sales opportunities, the prosecution of sales opportunities, and the management of customer issues.

The other software applications that orbit the CRM in the sales system are dependent on the CRM, either because their reason for existence is to feed it data (new contacts, perhaps) or because they leverage the data that sits within the CRM to perform specialist functions (e.g., email broadcast, report generation).

The CRM is a subset of a larger class of software, known as *enterprise resource planning* (ERP). ERP is the software that manages operational workflows in the organization as a whole. Things such as order generation, production environment scheduling, inventory management, payables and receivables processing, and so on.

Although ERP and CRM are now intertwined, the two technologies had quite different beginnings. ERP evolved out of the inventory control systems in the 1960s, and CRM evolved out of contact-tracking applications in the 1980s. Contact-tracking applications (e.g., Act!) were the software equivalents of salespeople's day-planner calendars.

Although the two technologies have grown together over the years, their usage has not. In the modern organization, ERP is pervasive; if you remove it, the organization would simply cease to function. This is not the case with the CRM. In fact, in many organizations, the removal of the CRM would actually unencumber salespeople and *increase* their productivity.

What's Wrong with the CRM?

Consider the list of standard promises made on behalf of CRM by CRM vendors:

- CRM will increase salespeople's productivity.
- CRM will cause an improvement in customer service quality.
- CRM will drive a tighter integration of sales and marketing.
- CRM will provide management with better quality information.

As I mentioned earlier, most organizations have invested a king's ransom in CRM, but few have seen any—let alone all—of these promises realized.

Technically, however, there is *nothing* wrong with the CRM!

As we'll shortly discover, the CRM has the potential to unleash enormous productivity improvements in sales environments. The problem with this technology is that it has been designed around the requirements of a sales environment that doesn't actually exist. It's useful (and somewhat amusing) to understand why this has occurred.

A Candid History of the CRM

It's arguable that the first contact-tracking applications solved a real problem for salespeople. These applications simplified the tracking of the numerous interactions between salespeople and their customers (appointments, phone calls, proposals, and other tasks).

I say *arguable*, because salespeople's legacy tool (their day-planner calendar) was actually superior to these applications for a couple of reasons: Calendars were, until very recently, much more portable than computers and did not take five minutes or so to switch on. And most salespeople did not share their calendars with management—meaning that they could make whatever entries they saw fit, without fear that the information would be used against them.

Understandably, because contact-tracking applications provided salespeople with some—but not a huge amount of—value, salespeople purchased them, though not in particularly large numbers.

This incursion of technology into the sales environment was observed with some interest by two groups of people: management and technologists. Managers were excited because they had witnessed the profound productivity improvements that had been delivered to production environments by ERP. And technologists were excited too; they had seen the unimaginable wealth generated by the ERP pioneers. In fact, the only party in the organization that wasn't particularly excited by CRM was salespeople. After their experiences with contact tracking, they were nonplussed by the breathless promises of management and the technologists.

It took the technologists only about fifteen years to transform those simple contact-tracking applications into technology that is as mature as ERP applications in almost every sense. And every step of the way, the technologists' progress was cheered by management, who fell over themselves to purchase each new iteration of the technology—despite the lack of any evidence of returns on their expenditure.

Unlike ERP which evolved around the requirements of real users, CRM has never really been embraced by users in any meaningful sense. Absent useful user feedback, technologists have had no choice but to design the technology around their vision of what a sales environment should look like. Hence my claim, previously, that CRM has been designed around an environment that doesn't actually exist.

The good news—and who'd have thought this story would end well—is that the environment that the technologists imagined is disarmingly similar to the environment evangelized in this book. Specifically, the technologists imagined an environment in which actors work as teams—rather than as autonomous agents—and engineered CRM around this idealized vision of reality.

I don't think this fortunate outcome is the result of incredible prescience on technologists' behalf—although, they do tend to be pretty smart critters; I think it's more that CRM has naturally inherited the architecture of ERP, which has collaboration in its genes.

Invalid Premise

This short history lesson should make it clear why CRM has consistently failed to deliver on its promises.

All those promises were premised on the existence of a team environment in sales. The 360-degree view of the customer—available to anyone in the organization—is of no value to anyone at all if the salesperson is working hard to monopolize the customer relationship (often with the customer aiding and abetting their cause). The technology to tightly integrate sales and marketing is of no value to anyone if sales and marketing are fundamentally distrustful of one another—and even less so if the two departments are held accountable to metrics that propel them apart. And the ability for management to see salespeople's efforts and outcomes is of no use if the salespeople have the power to flavor the data they enter into the CRM, along with huge incentives to do so. (These incentives emerge from the bizarre game that sales managers and their salespeople play in which both pretend that it's possible for salespeople to simultaneously be team members and autonomous agents.)

Sadly, many—perhaps most—salespeople have come to despise the software that originated as *their* productivity tool. The refrain—*CRM sucks*—is one that's frequently heard in the modern sales environment!

How Technology Can Add Real Value to Sales

Despite the many well-publicized problems that large organizations have had with the adoption of ERP, this technology has become indispensable to the modern corporation. The reason is that it facilitates the division of labor: It enables data to be shared across geography and departments in real time; it allows repetitive processes to be automated; and it allows management to extract information from oceans of data and consequently to make better decisions, faster.

These are exactly the benefits that the CRM and its associated technologies can provide to sales environments.

Sharing Data

In the inside-out model, it's critical that data be shared across both geography and departments. As we discussed earlier, customers expect a *single conversation* with your organization. Of course, this conversation has multiple participants (often in both yours and the customers' organizations), and those participants are in different locations and in different departments.

For example, in a complex sales environment, the conversation might consist of the following interactions:

- your field-based business-development manager (BDM) and your prospect's commercial decision makers;
- your BDM, their business-development coordinator, and your prospect's executive assistant;
- your project leader and your prospect's engineering team; or
- your customer service team and your prospect's operational people (assuming the prospect is an existing account).

The availability of data is a necessary condition for the synchronization of these interactions into a single conversation, but it's not a sufficient one. Sufficiency requires that each participant in this conversation is presented only with relevant data and that this data is presented in a meaningful way.

For example, a salesperson on their way to a meeting with one of your account's senior executives does need to know the general status of that account; however, they do not need a log of every transaction your organization has had with that account this year.

The CRM can assist with both of these conditions. Because the heart of the CRM is a giant database, the sharing of data is easy, but the CRM also makes it possible for you to provide different people in your organization—and even people in your client's organization—with custom views of the central data set.

So, in the example above, customer service representatives will see your account's discrete transactions, but when your salesperson scans their calendar in your client's reception area, they will see just a brief summary of sales volumes, the categories of products purchased, and your organization's on-time delivery performance.

Automation

Like all software, the CRM is brilliant at the automation of repetitive operations. At a basic level, the sharing of data is an example of automation. A single data element can be entered once and viewed by multiple parties in different locations without additional (human) effort.

Where promotion is concerned, there are more dramatic examples of automation: A prospective customer who completes a form on a landing page can be automatically subscribed to one or more automated communication programs, and the data they volunteer can be used to automatically populate company, contact, and opportunity records in your CRM. And with the push of a single button, personalized invitations to an event can be broadcast to thousands of contacts on your house list.

It's worth noting that the benefits of automation tend to be overhyped by CRM vendors. In a complex-sale environment, the automation of the opportunity-management process is the responsibility of a business-development coordinator—not of the CRM. If you have humans involved in the prosecution of sales opportunities (salespeople), it's safe to assume that it's impractical for this part of the overall sales process to be managed by a machine.

Management Information

We've already hinted at the distinction between data and information—and at the ability of CRM to convert the former into the latter. This distinction is particularly relevant to management. The design of the modern organization puts management in the position of wielding tremendous power—but this power can only be put to good use if management is presented with the right information at the right time.

The CRM stores data in a structure that makes the provision of this critical management information relatively easy, and the CRM (if it's used sensibly) gives management access to real-time reporting, eliminating the requirement for anyone in your organization to have to prepare standard reports.

YOUR GENERAL TECHNOLOGY REQUIREMENTS

Your technology requirements start with the CRM, but they probably don't end there. In all likelihood, you will need a number of technologies to power your entire sales function. Although many CRMs are billed as all-in-one solutions, it generally makes more sense to assemble a small collection of best-of-breed technologies. This is because all-in-one solutions tend to suffer either from missing functionality or from hideous complexity.

CRM

The power of CRM is its ability to model the complexity associated with both sales and customer support.

The landscape looks like the following. At the base level, we have our house list (accounts and potential accounts). We then have the initiatives that we perform that involve those accounts. Each initiative is a workflow, and each of those workflows consists of a sequence of events (e.g., phone calls, appointments, proposals).

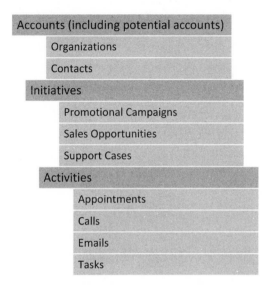

Figure 40. While other relationships tend to be supported, the most common CRM approach is to associate activities with initiatives, and initiatives with accounts.

All CRMs have this basic model hardwired into their architecture—which is a good thing, because this is exactly what reality looks like! This structure makes it easy for team members in various departments to enter and retrieve data, and it makes reporting easier too.

Your Website

Years ago, your website was a static document (brochureware). Today, it needs to be integrated (not necessarily in a technical sense) with many of your business functions and, for this reason, you need the flexibility to manage your website internally, rather than, for example, relying on a design firm. This means that even the simplest of websites should be built within a content-management system (CMS).

Where sales is concerned, your website will make a significant contribution to the generation of sales opportunities. In conjunction with search engines, it will doubtlessly generate some sales opportunities organically but, more importantly, most (if not all) of your promotional activities will drive prospective customers to your website, where they will complete forms on custom landing pages, which are likely to be among the most frequently edited content on your website.

Lead-Management (Marketing Automation) Systems

In recent years, a particularly valuable class of software has emerged to bridge the divide between your website (or, more specifically, your landing pages) and your CRM. *Lead-management* (or *marketing automation*) software consists of a class of web-based applications that provide the following functionality:

- form design and hosting (e.g., those that appear in your landing pages),
- contact list management (the data that's collected when prospects submit forms),
- autoresponders (sequences of automated email messages), and
- mass email broadcast functions.

Applications that bill themselves as *marketing automation* tend to target the enterprise market with total solutions that include features such as website analytics, landing page hosting (rather than just forms), and the ability to build quite sophisticated automated communications around a range of prospect behaviors (e.g., web browsing history, links followed from emails, forms completed).

Management Information System

Your next requirement is for a management information system (MIS). Most CRMs come with reporting capabilities, but in many cases, it makes sense to use a discrete MIS because more often than not, you will want reports that merge data from multiple sources (e.g., the CRM, ERP, and web analytics services), because each level of management will have quite different information requirements, and because less is more (i.e., it is not beneficial for a manager to have to browse hundreds of reports to find the two or three that are relevant to them).

CHOOSING SPECIFIC TECHNOLOGIES

I'm sure you won't forgive me if I make some specific technology recommendations! However, because this advice will age quickly, it will undoubtedly be worth paying more attention to the reasons for my recommendations than to the recommendations themselves.

CRM

In line with my earlier comment about the danger of all-in-one solutions, my first piece of advice is to avoid purchasing the CRM that is provided by your ERP vendor.

You should avoid this for two simple reasons:

1. you will likely make significant sacrifices in the areas of functionality and (importantly) usability;
2. the tight integration that your vendor promises will come at the expense of terrible complexity.

It's important to stress that, in the inside-out model, tight integration of ERP and the CRM is not required. This is because your division of labor means that different people will require different data or different views of the same data. As was mentioned earlier, your salesperson, for example, doesn't need access to transactional data; they just need a summary view of this data.

The only data that does require relatively tight integration is address book data—and this can certainly be achieved without purchasing an all-in-one solution. Similarly, your other integration requirements, such as the salesperson's transaction summary, can be achieved either at the reporting level or with low-cost add-ins.

My second piece of advice, where the CRM is concerned, is that the core technology is relatively mature, meaning that the differences between CRMs are minimal and tend to diminish with each new release.

For this reason, I recommend that you give special consideration to

- the size of the support community (and the availability of third-party plug-ins),
- the ease of customization, and
- the price.

With these considerations in mind, let me tell you our three current recommendations:

Vtiger

Vtiger is an open-source application, meaning that you can download it and host it yourself and that customization is very easy. It has a decent-size support community and tons of functionality, and it's very easy to use. The downside is that it's not well known (unlike the next recommendation).

Salesforce

Salesforce is the Rolls Royce of CRMs. It has every feature known to mankind and comes with an enormous support community. It's also a user-friendly application (although there is a learning curve). The downside is that it's expensive—*really damn expensive*—particularly if you want to integrate it with third-party services! Bear in mind that this expense is not just a barrier to purchasing Salesforce. We often see organizations that have committed to Salesforce because of its enormous capabilities but who are then reluctant to exploit those capabilities because of the per-user license cost associated with introducing new team members to the platform.

Microsoft CRM

Microsoft CRM is the obvious choice for those organizations that have made a big commitment to the Microsoft enterprise environment because of its out-of-the-box interoperability with SharePoint and other MS services. It's a feature-rich and user-friendly application, particularly for users who are used to the MS environment.

❄ ❄ ❄ ❄

The inside-out model does make two critical requirements of CRM that you should be mindful of: MS Exchange or Google Apps integration and batch generation of sales opportunities.

Because field salespeople spend all their time in the field, it's critical that your CRM push appointments into your salespeople's mobile devices (not just into their Outlook calendars). This tends to require either MS Exchange (not Outlook) integration or Google Apps integration. Be warned: Most CRM salespeople are less than truthful where this requirement is concerned!

In the inside-out model, sales opportunities are generated by promotions and not by salespeople. Because promotional campaigns tend to target batches of prospects, it's important that your campaign coordinator be able to autogenerate a sales opportunity for each campaign recipient. MS CRM is the only CRM that I'm aware of that comes with this functionality. Ballistix (a company I founded) has written plug-ins for Salesforce and Vtiger (and other CRMs) to achieve this.

Website

The choice of website and content management is easy. The most popular content-management system with the biggest support community and the richest feature set (by a country mile) also happens to be free—WordPress. Like Vtiger, WordPress is open source.

Do not, under any circumstances, allow a web developer to sell you their in-house CMS or—worse still—to build you a custom website from the ground up. Even if you have special requirements (for example, the integration of operational data into your website), you're still better off building a website on the WordPress platform and then integrating your operational data at the few points where it is really required; in many cases, this can be achieved by pasting a snippet of JavaScript into your WordPress page editor.[17]

Lead-Management (Marketing Automation) Applications

As was mentioned, lead-management applications are all web applications nowadays. You have the services that bill themselves as lead management—our pick of these is Aweber—and those that offer the full marketing-automation solution—a good example of these is Marketo.

My advice is to start with Aweber and avoid expensive marketing-automation applications until you are convinced there is a good business case for upgrading. If you use Aweber in conjunction with WordPress, Google Analytics (see the next section), and a third-party CRM plug-in, you'll find that you can enjoy most of the features of a marketing-automation application at a fraction of the cost.

In case you're wondering, I'm suggesting Aweber rather than MailChimp and other contenders because Aweber has an invaluable feature that enables you to create multiple sequences of automated emails and then automatically move prospects from one sequence to the next as they complete forms on your landing pages. For example, you might have a first-time visitor watch a video and prompt them for an email address one-third of the way in (there's a WordPress plug-in for this). The receipt of that email address might trigger a sequence of automated emails that encourages the visitor to request a document of some kind, and each email would provide a link to a new landing page the visitor can use to do so.

When the visitor requests the document, they would be automatically unsubscribed from the first email sequence and subscribed to a new one. This new sequence might encourage the visitor to express interest in a conference call with one of your salespeople and, again, would provide a link to another landing page the visitor can use to accept this offer.

As an aside, I would encourage you to mark automated emails as such. The reason is that the most effective emails are the ones your prospect could easily believe you custom generated for them. It is best to aim for the most effective emails possible and to simultaneously ensure that no one will be deceived.

Management Information System

Those who love purchasing new technology will be disappointed by my recommendation here. In my opinion, the most valuable reporting tool—hands down—is Excel. More specifically, the pivot table (and pivot chart) functionality within Excel. It's true that CRM and ERP systems come with reporting capabilities, but the problem is that the data you wish to report on often live in different locations (e.g., ERP, the CRM, and online services).

To convert Excel into a full-blown management information system, all you need to do is find a way to import the data on which you wish to report into Excel, and then show management how to drive a pivot table (or pivot chart).

Fortunately, both are relatively easy. The most elegant way to achieve the former is to organize for a technical person to make the data on which you wish to report available to you as password-protected XML feeds (one feed for each data set). Excel can easily digest these feeds and allow you to manipulate them to your heart's content in a pivot table (or pivot chart).

Conceptually, pivot tables are difficult to comprehend, but managers tend to take to them like ducks to water once they see them in action. This is because they are incredibly powerful and because you can quickly assemble the reports you want with a combination of drag and drop and trial and error.

Imagine that Mary's colleagues have requested a report that compares her firm's return on investment on LinkedIn and Facebook advertising. She will request access to three data sets from IT:

- cost-per-click data from LinkedIn and Facebook (these can easily be merged into one table);
- opportunity data from CRM (this will enable Mary to see the opportunities generated from online campaigns, as well as whether they go on to become customers); and
- monthly customer expenditure data from ERP.

IT will provide Mary with an Excel workbook with each of these data sets in a table on its own sheet. Mary can then generate a number of pivot tables, each referencing one or more of those data sets (Excel will prompt her to identify common fields in each data set that can be used to join the three tables).

Mary might start by creating a pivot table that lists customers that originated from each of those promotional sources. She can then create a second table that compares Facebook and LinkedIn expenditure with the total sales generated by customers originating from those sources.

The beauty of this report (figure 41) is that once Mary has access to that raw data, she can answer most questions without additional recourse to IT. This is in contrast to alternative approaches to management information, which tend to make management dependent on the IT department for every change they wish to make to their reports.

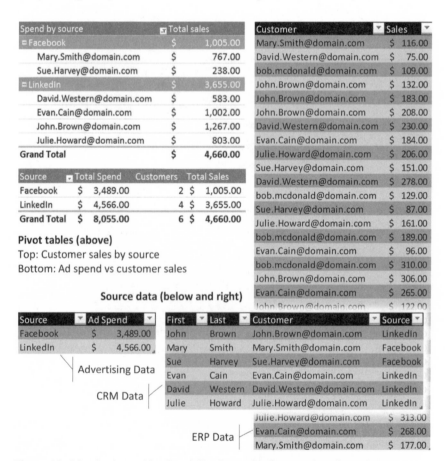

Figure 41. Mary's pivot tables (top left), along with the raw data (from three sources) she used to create them (with minimal help from IT).

THE IMPORTANCE OF IN-HOUSE TECHNICAL CAPABILITY

I'm a big fan of open-source applications. Obviously the fact that most of these applications are free contributes to my enthusiasm—but this is only the beginning.

I believe that open-source applications make a lot of sense for two important reasons: With any major application (ERP or CRM), you will save enough on license fees to employ (at least) one full-time developer to work on the application for you, and these applications are extremely easy to modify and to integrate with other applications, meaning that your in-house developer will enable you to get incredible mileage from limited technology expenditure.

Now, it's quite likely that you may not find the idea of employing a full-time developer appealing. It's tempting to conclude that it will make more sense to purchase a commercial application from a (value-added) reseller, who can then provide you with ongoing technical support.

In my experience, where a small-to-medium enterprise is concerned, this conclusion is wrong. The harsh reality is that to extract real value from enterprise technology, you simply must have in-house technical capability. In almost every case, those organizations I work with that depend on third-party technology providers discover that their enterprise technology becomes an incredibly expensive bottleneck.

The problem is that the economics of a value-added reseller (in the small-to-medium enterprise space) prevent those firms from developing a detailed understanding of their customers' businesses and prevent them from being as agile as is necessary to really add value.

EMBRACING TECHNOLOGY

But there's another reason my position on open-source makes sense: Building your own in-house technical capability is the third step in my three steps to embracing technology.

It's worth pausing for a minute to consider the role technology plays in business in general. One view is that technology allows us to simplify or automate activities, but this view would lead us to conclude that technology is a tactical consideration only, and this conclusion would be wrong.

Throughout history, there have been a number of advances in technology that are so significant that they fundamentally change the way business is conducted—as opposed to simply automating an activity or two. In recent times, information technology seems to have resulted in these fundamental changes occurring at an increased rate, as is evidenced by the effects of Amazon on retail, iTunes on music, E-Trade on stockbroking, and so on.

The result is that it's exceptionally dangerous, in my opinion, to make strategic decisions without a sound understanding of technology. And, if you're the business owner or a senior executive, it needs to be *you* with that sound understanding—not a board member, partner, or employee. Your understanding of technology needs to be deep enough to enable you to appreciate the implications of technology implicitly and deep enough to enable you to communicate effectively with technical people.

If you're not sure where you rank in your tech fluency, I've composed a set of three questions you can use to make your own evaluation. To answer these questions, you need a reasonably deep understanding of technology, rather than just the ability to decipher a technical acronym or two.

- What is a relational database, and what would a nonrelational database look like?
- What is multitier architecture, and what problems does it solve?
- What is the essence of the *agile* approach to software development, and in what environment might the agile approach not make sense?

If you struggle to answer these questions, I have a solution for you—in three steps. Sadly, it's not a quick fix; it's more of a journey. But, I do think it's a journey well worth embarking on. (Remember, software engineers have a history of mastering business faster than businesspeople tend to master technology!)

1. Read about the history of technology. This is a great way of gaining an appreciation of technology fundamentals (which rarely change). Read biographies of Alan Turing and John von Neumann; read about the history of Xerox PARC and about the history of algorithms.

2. Get your feet wet. Create a simple database-based application for yourself—from scratch. Use Microsoft Access or Zoho Creator to create a personal expense tracker, a catalogue of your wine collection, or an application to track your exercise or food consumption. MS Access and Zoho Creator are great, because you can make good initial progress with simple drag-and-drop functionality before you're inevitably forced to write a line or two of code. (Yep, I'm serious, I'm actually expecting you to write some code!)

3. Get some in-house development capability. Now that you're attacking your neophytism in a pincer move, you can strike a decisive blow by employing your first developer.

If you've taken my advice and installed one or more open-source applications, you can employ an engineer with broad experience in the LAMP stack (Google it!). Otherwise, it might make more sense to employ a technical project manager and have them outsource your coding requirements. If you've never managed a development specialist before, you'll discover that this is no small undertaking. Nonetheless, it's a lesson that needs to be learned.

By the way, if you have a third-party technology service provider, it makes a hell of a lot of sense to have this firm recruit your in-house person and assist you with their management. This will be money well spent! Finally, if you are a small-to-medium enterprise, and you have an IT systems administrator, you should definitely keep systems administration at arm's length from software development; these two functions have radically different world views, and they tend to be antagonistic.

I hope I've sold you on the point that technology is an executive leadership responsibility—not something to be delegated, at least not in its entirety. Either way, our discussion of technology has delivered us at the feet of management, the subject of our very last chapter.

Chapter 12
MANAGING THE SALES FUNCTION

When executives are first introduced to sales process engineering (SPE), they naturally assume that this new approach to sales will be tough on salespeople. But, interestingly, it tends not to be. Salespeople adapt quickly. They enjoy working in an environment that's custom-engineered to multiply their productivity.

The individual who really suffers as a result of this transition is the sales manager. Although the sales manager may approve of SPE in theory, in practice, they find themselves presiding over an environment they no longer understand and, as a consequence, an environment they are ill equipped to manage. Without executive foresight, this is likely to result in the sales function becoming rudderless at the very time you are trying to chart a new course.

In this final chapter, I discuss the management requirements of the inside-out model and the special requirements of the transition to SPE.

WHY DOES MANAGEMENT EXIST?

It doesn't hurt to start our discussion by reminding ourselves why management exists. We touched on this in chapter 2, when we recognized that the division of labor creates the requirement for management. When team members narrow their focus to a tiny subset of tasks, the responsibility for the synchronization of the environment as a whole needs to shift elsewhere.

Enter the manager!

In practice, managers tend to be responsible for more than just the internal synchronization of their functions. They are also responsible for maintaining the integrity of their domains, which translates into practical activities such as hiring and firing, controlling expenses, ensuring procedural compliance, and so on, and they are responsible for managing the interface between their functions and other organizational functions.

In the modern organization, management has become stratified: All but the smallest organizations evolve three levels of management, each with quite a different set of responsibilities:

- line management: the direct management of individual contributors (supervision),
- functional management: the management of a department, and
- executive management: responsible for long-range decision making and the architecture of the organization.

Management and the Traditional Model

In traditional environments, we tend to encounter managers at both the functional and executive levels.[18] If the organization is large enough to have an executive-level manager with sales responsibility (e.g., a VP of sales and marketing), we typically find that these individuals are very capable and ideally placed to champion the transition to the inside-out model.

However, where functional managers are concerned (the standard-issue sales manager), we tend to find that these individuals are either quite poor or quite exceptional—and they rarely fall anyplace in between!

We have the design of the traditional model to blame for this. As we've discussed previously, the hallmark of the traditional model is that salespeople operate as autonomous agents. Of course, autonomous salespeople and sales managers are two incompatible concepts. Salespeople either march to the beat of their own drums or they don't.

Sales managers develop two methods for coping with this conundrum.

The first and most common method is to avoid managing salespeople in the traditional sense of the word. The sales manager who adopts this approach tries to become established as a coach or a trusted advisor to salespeople. When there's a requirement for the sales manager to exercise some control, the manager will attempt to exchange some of the goodwill they have established with salespeople for a concession or two. They'll call in a favor, in other words.

The second method is to pay lip service to salespeople's autonomy but to ignore it in practice. The manager who adopts this approach will use the force of their personality to overpower their team members' autonomous ideals and rule them with a mix of fear and grudging respect.

Sadly, a manager who has adopted the first method will find the transition to the inside-out model very difficult (if not impossible). Unfortunately, their history with the sales team has resulted in the establishment of a number of negative precedents. Even if salespeople can put these precedents behind them, the sales manager very often can't.

The best approach, therefore, is to transition the sales manager into another role. If the sales manager was awarded the position because they were a capable salesperson, it may make sense for them to return to sales (and this will often actually be their preference).

A sales manager who has adopted the second method is well placed to transition to the inside-out model and will often be a major advocate of the new direction. The danger with these individuals is that their firebrand tendencies can often spill over into their interactions with other functions, poisoning the organization as a whole.

If you have a sales manager who is mature enough to rule their team like a tyrant and to interface with other departments like a diplomat, this individual is a rare find indeed and should probably be on the fast track to the executive suite!

MANAGEMENT REQUIREMENTS OF THE INSIDE-OUT MODEL

The inside-out model is structurally different from the traditional one—and this tends to have quite an impact on management requirements. For example, the centralization of customer service, and of a significant number of sales activities, results in a larger phone-based team. That team will benefit enormously from close supervision; in addition, the reduction in size of the field team and the elimination of most (if not all) regional sales offices will significantly reduce the political challenges associated with the management of a traditional sales team. As a result, the centralization of the generation of opportunities, along with the more sophisticated promotional function that's required to achieve this, will increase the complexity of the overall sales machine.

In summary, then, the transition to the inside-out model will tend to result in: a requirement for line management that didn't previously exist; a requirement for fewer functional managers (and with all sales activities centrally scheduled, silos cease to exist); and a significant increase in the scope of functional management or the emergence of a requirement for executive management (the head of sales is now managing a more complex machine).

The Boundaries of the Sales Function

It's hard to progress this discussion without first defining the boundaries of sales. Specifically, we need to consider whether customer service, marketing, and project leadership are to be considered part of the sales function. My short answers for each of these are, respectively, *sometimes*, *mostly*, and *never*.

Technically, customer service should be regarded as part of operations, not part of sales. The processing of repeat transactions, the generation of quotes, and the resolution of issues are all operational activities. However, customer service operators work in an environment very similar to that of inside sales personnel. They work in cubicles, illuminated by the glow of computer monitors, and they spend most of their time talking with customers via their headsets. This means, in practice, that unless your customer service team is large enough to warrant its own dedicated supervisor, it makes sense to integrate customer service with your other phone-based sales personnel. This way, you can justify adding a capable inside sales supervisor to manage the team as a whole.

Where marketing is concerned, either some or all of marketing should live within sales and, again, size is the main consideration. It's useful to consider marketing as two discrete functions. There's marketing communications (or *marcoms*, as it's typically called) and promotions. The former involves the preparation of general communication materials, the maintenance of web properties, investor relations, and so on; and the latter involves the execution of promotional campaigns expressly designed to maintain your sales team's opportunity queues. The former is primarily concerned with communications infrastructure and is typically engaged in longer-lead-time initiatives. The latter scrambles to run campaigns and replenish fast-depleting opportunity queues. The two functions have different perspectives and operate at quite different cadences.

Our position is that promotions should always be a part of sales and that marcoms may or may not be, depending on the size of that function. In a small organization, it's likely that the promotions would consist of just a campaign coordinator (and, most likely, a part-time research analyst) and that all other marketing would be outsourced. In a larger organization, the promotions team might contain a number of specialists (e.g., campaign coordinators, research analysts, event coordinators, data analysts), and this team would likely commission all necessary inputs from the marketing department (marcoms).

So, for the purpose of our discussion, we'll treat (just) promotions as part of the sales function, although we will drop in on marketing again when we discuss executive management.

Project leaders must be neither a part of sales nor a part of production. As we discussed earlier, their very reason for existence is, in part, to manage the necessary tension between these two functions. Accordingly, project leaders can belong to your engineering function if you have one; and if you don't, project leadership should be a department of its own (assuming you need it, of course).

Line Management

If you have a team of phone-based operators (customer service, inside sales, and business-development coordinators), a capable supervisor can have a significant impact on the team's overall productivity. Of course, in the inside-out model, you will quickly assemble such a team and, because you are centralizing your internal team members, it will be possible for you to justify a capable supervisor in short order. It will make sense for this supervisor to manage your entire internal sales team, including your campaign coordinator, research analysts, and customer service representatives, until your customer service team is large enough to warrant its own supervisor.

In short, your internal sales supervisor should be responsible for the following metrics:

- for customer service, on-time case completion (relative to targets for each case type);
- for the campaign coordinator, opportunity queue sizes (relative to optimal);
- for inside sales, throughput (daily or weekly sales); and
- for the business-development coordinator, the business-development manager's (BDM's) number of forward-booked days (utilization).

Where sales is concerned, a necessary condition is activity volume. This means that the supervisor should obsess over the volume of meaningful selling interactions. As the sales function grows, you can allocate dedicated supervisors, first to customer service and then to promotions. Because the research analyst role consists of repetitive, mostly phone-based work, it's better to have your research analyst supervised by the inside sales supervisor, although the content of their work should still be determined by promotions.

The sensitive question now is who manages the field salespeople. Well, of course, in the inside-out model, you are likely to have only a fraction of the field salespeople you had previously, which means that it's quite likely that your field team is nowhere near large enough to justify a field supervisor. This means that your field salespeople will need to answer to whoever is leading the sales function as a whole.

Functional Management

As I suggested earlier, we can see that the sales manager's domain looks quite different in this new model. In the traditional model, the sales manager oversaw a group of field salespeople—and that was about it. Now, however, our sales manager has a much smaller number of field-based reports, and the rest of their team is inside. This inside team contains three quite distinct specialties (and four additional subspecialties).

And, as has been a central theme of this whole book, in the inside-out model, sales functions quite differently. Sales is now a machine—and the success of that machine is more a function of its internal coordination than it is of individual feats of heroism. This requires a different approach to management: more *lieutenant colonel* and less *Wolf of Wall Street.*

As you may already suspect, in a smaller organization, the requirement for both an inside sales supervisor and a sales manager is questionable. It might be better, in these circumstances, either to have a sales manager manage the entire sales function (including promotions and customer service) or to have no sales manager at all and have the field personnel answer directly to a senior executive.

If you do not already have a capable sales manager, with a sales function of this size, the latter would be preferable. It is certainly less risky to employ a supervisor for the inside team and to have a senior executive (ideally the CEO) manage field personnel than it is to gamble on a sales manager. This is particularly true if you are in the process of transitioning from the old model to the inside-out model. A new sales manager is much more likely to try to recreate their previous sales environment than they are to dutifully build the environment described in a book that they agreed (somewhat reluctantly) to read during the recruiting process!

Executive Management

As I mentioned earlier, larger organizations will typically have a VP of sales (or a VP of sales and marketing). In smaller organizations, this responsibility typically rests on the shoulders of the CEO. Such a person is responsible for the overall design of the sales function and the integration of the sales function with the organization as a whole.

In a midsize organization, one that has grown large enough to justify this position, I would suggest expanding the scope of this role to include the whole growth value chain—specifically, new product development (NPD), marketing, and sales.

This is important because sales cannot continue to function effectively for any reasonable period without the tight integration of NPD and promotions. The absence of this integration is one of the most common (and persistent) problems I see with midsize to large organizations.

Accordingly, my preference would be to title the executive-management role *VP of growth* or something similar.

Conclusion

In summary, then, if you are transitioning your organization from the traditional to the inside-out model—and if your sales function is small but growing—I would expect to see the following:

You will commence by adding a supervisor to oversee your fast-growing internal team (inside sales, promotions, and customer service). Your CEO will assume responsibility for general sales management and for the direct management of your field-based salespeople. This is likely to require that your CEO perform occasional high-value sales calls to assist your field salespeople with major opportunities. Your CEO will also fill the role of VP of growth, which requires that they take a special interest in NPD.

As you grow, you will add a customer service supervisor, and you will nominate a team leader within your promotions team (the campaign coordinator). At some point, your CEO will add a sales manager, so they can take a backseat in functional management responsibilities (including joint calls with salespeople and running regular sales meetings).

Ultimately, your CEO might choose to hand off the VP of growth responsibilities, or they may prefer to hand off other responsibilities and maintain focus on this critical role.

How to Manage Sales

What follows is a general discussion of how to manage sales. This section contains advice for both supervisors and functional managers. Effective sales management starts with a decision to manage—in the true sense of the word—and this, for many managers and executives, is the toughest decision of all. In the inside-out model, the manager must shoulder a number of responsibilities that have traditionally been delegated to salespeople.

In the traditional model, salespeople are responsible for generating sales, and sales managers are responsible for supporting them to the extent they need support (and for staying out of their way when they don't).

In the inside-out model, because sales is now a team sport, it is no longer possible for salespeople to single-handedly generate sales—any more than it is possible for a single football player to win a game. This means that management, rather than salespeople, must own the responsibility for sales outcomes, and management must be responsible for both the overall design and the day-to-day supervision of each of the components of the sales machine.

Preconditions for Sales Management

A decision to manage isn't the only precondition. The following are also critical requirements:

- a goal and a set of necessary conditions,
- an understanding of the dynamics of the sales machine,
- a management method, and
- management information.

Goal and Necessary Conditions

In chapter 4, we looked at how most modern organizations benefit from the system constraint being maintained (by sales) upstream from either production (make to order) or engineering (engineer to order). In these circumstances, the goal of sales *should not be to sell as much as possible!* The goal should be to maintain the size of the order book within an acceptable range. Sales management must know exactly the number of days' worth of work (and the mix of work) that should be maintained in this buffer, and, of course, the sales machine must be engineered with these requirements in mind.

In addition to the goal, sales management must have an explicit understanding of the necessary conditions—conditions that must be maintained in order for the achievement of the goal to be valid. For example, sales management needs to know the *allowable acquisition cost*—the maximum that can be spent on promotion in order to win a new account.

Dynamics of the Sales Machine

Obviously, it's not possible to manage a machine unless you understand its inner workings. Accordingly, sales management must have a profound understanding of the entire sales and promotion value chain. They should understand the often circuitous path that $1 in promotional spending follows in order to be transformed into an account worth thousands—or tens of thousands—of dollars in lifetime value.

They should also understand that theirs is not an infinite-capacity environment. They should appreciate that each team member has a maximum sustainable capacity, and that most, if not all, should not be allowed to operate at full capacity for extended periods of time.

Management Method

The organization as a whole should have a formal approach to management—a standard process and a set of minimal requirements. Sales, obviously, should inherit this method. In the unhappy event that the organization doesn't have one, sales management will have to lead by example.

My preference is that this method be simple. It should require that management participate in a small number of regular—and high-value—meetings, and it should pay as much attention to what managers *don't* do as to what they *do* do! Specifically, managers should *always* have protective capacity; a fully burdened manager is an ineffective manager.

Management Information

It should be obvious that management needs data in order to manage. A manager without data is a fool with an ego (and, as far as fools go, the ones with egos tend to be the most insufferable!). When I declared above that management must have a profound understanding of the sales value chain, the word *profound* was intended to indicate that management is required to understand the cause-and-effect relationships within the sales function *at a mathematical level.*

The management information system should take two forms. It should provide sales data in a form that enables management to ask questions of it (hence my love of pivot tables).[19] And it should allow the manager to expose whatever (small number of) metrics it makes sense for team members to be focusing on at any given moment in time.

In my opinion, sales management cannot get by without a basic (high-school level) understanding of statistics. If your sales manager does not have this, you must insist that they remedy this problem immediately. A sales manager without an understanding of statistics is like a chef who lacks an appreciation for food hygiene; both will look the part, but no good will come of either in the long run.

Line Management: Managing Salespeople

Now that we have those management preconditions in place, let's talk about how to actually manage salespeople (inside and field salespeople). I propose a three-step formula: conviction, activity, and deals.

Conviction

Your sales manager must start with the conviction that your offering is salable and that it can reasonably be sold by your sales team. I don't mean fake conviction. I mean the kind of quiet conviction that comes from certainty, as in *I'm convinced the sun will rise tomorrow.*

Once your sales manager has this conviction, they must ensure that at least the opinion leaders within your sales team have it too. Now, you don't get this conviction by faking it. You get it by proving—beyond reasonable doubt—that your offering is actually salable and that it can be sold by your sales team!

If the opinion leaders within your sales team lack this conviction, your sales manager must make calls with them, initially, to demonstrate how it is done and then, ultimately, to ensure that they do it successfully.

If your sales manager lacks this conviction, guess what: You must make calls with them, initially, to demonstrate how it is done and then, ultimately, to ensure that they do it successfully.

If you are a VP of sales, this is a responsibility that you clearly can't dodge. Similarly, if you are a product manager, the CEO, or the founder, the buck stops with you! Shine your shoes, install your sales manager in the jump seat, and go make some sales (either in person or by phone).

I'm serious.

If you are a senior executive, you should be able to sell a salable proposition simply by virtue of your seniority, and if you're the founder, you shouldn't even need to shine your shoes—a clean pair of running shoes should be sufficient! If you're a senior executive (or the founder) and *you* can't sell your offering, you'd better face reality: Your offering is *not* salable, your system constraint is not in sales, and you're reading the wrong book![20]

Conviction is important because without it, your sales manager has no authority and simply cannot manage.

Do not skip this step.

Activity

We've already discussed that activity—or more specifically, *meaningful selling conversations*—is the primary driver of sales. Activity alone doesn't guarantee you sales, but an absence of activity is a guarantee of an absence of sales. For this reason, the sales manager should treat activity as a necessary condition. Each salesperson must perform a fixed volume of sales activity, day in and day out.

If we're dealing with field salespeople, this is more of a process- than a people-management issue. In the inside-out model, it's the responsibility of promotions, in conjunction with business-development coordinators, to ensure that the BDM's calendars are fully booked (four appointments a day, five days a week). Typically you'll find that if field salespeople wake each day to discover a day full of prescheduled meetings, they will be quite happy to perform them. During the transition to the inside-out model, management may need to act to ensure that salespeople do not quarantine working hours for personal or off-grid business activities.

Where inside salespeople are concerned, it's critical that your sales manager stipulate an optimum daily volume of meaningful selling conversations, as well as an allowable range. Generally in an inside sales environment, this will be somewhere north of thirty meaningful conversations a day. In such an environment, a meaningful selling conversation should be defined as any conversation in which the sales proposition is discussed, as opposed to a simple connect or an agreement to call back later.

If inside salespeople use email or chat to sell, you might like to use the term *meaningful selling interaction*. Either way, all interactions should be tracked in the customer relationship management application (CRM) and coded to enable interactions of the meaningful variety to be counted.

It's important to note that activity volume is a necessary condition, not the goal. Accordingly, it should be expected and not celebrated. The only exception is when you are attempting to shift to a new activity level.

In inside sales environments, there are a couple of techniques you can use to ensure consistent activity volumes: protected calling blocks—periods of time (typically one-hour blocks) during which the team sprints to achieve a minimum volume of meaningful conversations; and the *desk-is-for-working* rule—a stipulation that, if the salesperson is at their desk, they are on the phone. (It is not a stipulation that the salesperson should spend all day at their desk, however.) I like both of these techniques because they recognize that people are not robots; they perform best when they can sprint and then relax.

The inside sales team of one of our silent revolutionaries (in Australia) works in a mezzanine above their plant. All the sales team members like to lift weights (as do I), and they have a mini gym on the plant floor beneath where they work. Their sales manager's rule is that working hours are either for banging out calls or squeezing out reps—either is fine by him (and by me)!

Deals

If your salespeople have conviction—and if activity levels are consistently high—deals will flow. If you'd like them to flow faster, then and only then should you turn your attention to sales techniques (e.g., skill development).

Actually, I should say, when all sales performance prerequisites are in place, your sales manager *must* work with all salespeople on skill development (at least weekly). The only time that a salesperson should be excused from sales drills is if management agrees that they are a sales master and if their relative sales performance is consistently in the fourth quartile.

I use the term *drills* deliberately. Day-to-day sales training should be similar in design to athletic or military training, as opposed to classroom-style instruction. In addition, this day-to-day training should be the responsibility of your sales manager. Sales drills should consist primarily of role-playing exercises. Role-playing is analogous to sparring in boxing and other fighting arts. The objective is to build muscle memory, to convert exchanges that might otherwise feel unnatural into natural reflexes. Repetition is the key to mastery.

In most cases, it is impractical to script entire sales conversations (the obvious exceptions are appointment-setting calls). My preference, instead, is to divide the ideal selling conversation into a set of steps and script the transitions (or *bridges*) between steps (including asking for the order).[21]

During the drills, the scripted portions of sales exchanges should be delivered word for word, following the script; that's the reason for the script in the first place! Normalizing the words enables the team to focus its attention on their delivery.

On Sales Managers Who Don't

Now, I know that most sales managers don't manage like this. And, to some extent, that's understandable. After all, in the traditional model, salespeople are supposed to be autonomous. But that does not alter my conviction that this is how you manage salespeople. It's how I was managed when I joined the insurance industry many years ago, and it's how I managed my own team of salespeople. Then, when I advanced to a head of sales position, it's how I insisted my sales managers manage their teams. (In spite of the fact that our salespeople were technically autonomous, we didn't allow that to prevent us from terrorizing them into making stupendous amounts of money!)

To be frank, I'm horrified by what passes for sales management in most organizations I visit today. The truth is that most sales managers meet with their teams infrequently, deliver no training, and spend most of their time on their own sales calls.

The inside-out model provides sales managers with both information and control; it's absolutely critical that they embrace both, and it's absolutely critical that you insist they do!

Performance Is Not Optional!

On the subject of assuming control, one of the benefits of eliminating sales commissions is that it enables management to make it clear that performance is not optional.

If a salesperson is on your team, they must sell to stay there (just as a welder on your shop floor must weld). It's true that sales is a more uncertain environment than production, but that's why it's important that your sales manager possess a highschool-level understanding of statistics. Statistics provides the tools your manager needs to collapse the uncertainty and arrive at certain assessments of an individual's performance.

The easiest way to evaluate salespeople's performance is to calculate the throughput (contribution margin) they generate, on average, for each meaningful conversation they perform. You can then compare individual salespeople with their colleagues.

The benefit of assessing salespeople on a relative basis is that it allows you to control for factors outside their influence (e.g., the efficacy of promotional campaigns, your estimating team's pricing policies, and so on).

Sales Management Mechanics

Because sales management is a supervisory (line-management) role, the manager should be colocated with—and work closely with—their team. They should not own any sales opportunities, and they should not perform any calls or appointments unless they are doing it in the company of one of their salespeople. As should be the case with all managers, most of your sales manager's time should be unscheduled. They cannot effectively supervise their team if they are busy.

Aside from general (deliberately) unstructured supervision, your sales manager (and all line managers) should perform the following:

- a daily stand-up work-in-progress (WIP) meeting—more on that in a minute;
- periodic one-on-one discussions with team members;
- joint calls with field salespeople (or joint-calling sessions with inside salespeople); and
- recruiting.

Supervising the Internal Sales and Customer Service Personnel

As I discussed earlier, it often makes sense to combine inside sales, customer service, and business-development coordinators into one internal sales function. This results in a large enough team to justify the addition of a dedicated sales manager.

Managing the Sales Function

As is suggested by the title of this book, the sales function is a complex machine. This machine contains multiple teams of specialists: promotions, inside sales, business-development coordinators, field salespeople, and supervisors—and, sometimes, customer service.

The head of sales is responsible for ensuring both the internal and external synchronization of this machine. *Internal synchronization* means ensuring that these various teams work in harmony, and *external synchronization* means ensuring that the sales function integrates effectively with engineering, production, finance, and other departments.

External synchronization was discussed briefly in chapter 4, when I introduced Goldratt's theory of constraints (TOC). The basic idea is to start with an understanding of which of your departments is supposed to be your organization's constraint and then to make resource allocation decisions to ensure that it stays that way. For example, in a make-to-order environment, the role of both engineering and sales is to maintain an optimal-size order book upstream from manufacturing. This means that sales and engineering need protective capacity (enough capacity to sell and engineer at a faster rate than production can produce). It also means that these functions should ease off when the order book is full and sprint as it starts to diminish in size.

Internally, it makes sense to apply a similar programming approach to sales. In short, this involves nominating a team as the internal pacesetting resource (a virtual constraint), ensuring that other teams subordinate to the pacesetting resource, and maintaining a buffer of work upstream from the pacesetting resource and exploiting this buffer as a source of management information.

It makes the most sense for your internal pacesetting resource to be either your field-based salespeople or your inside sales team—typically the latter if you have both. This means that promotions and business-development coordinators should be responsible for ensuring that queues of work upstream from salespeople are maintained at their optimal sizes and that other teams process their work quickly to ensure that they don't become bottlenecks.

If you have read *The Goal* (Goldratt's master work), the preceding passage will make sense. If you have not, I urge you to remedy that urgently! Sadly, a comprehensive introduction to TOC in general—and the drum–buffer–rope approach to planning, in particular—is beyond the scope of this book.

Manage for Consistency, Not Peak Output

You may have noticed that this discussion elevates synchronization above the pursuit of peak results.

One colossal mistake we made back in my sales-management days was that we managed sales for peak output. We'd run regular sales competitions (sometimes with offers of overseas holidays for members of the winning team), and we'd congratulate ourselves on our ability to hit new sales highs as our promotions became more elaborate and our prizes more generous (and expensive).

In retrospect, though, it's clear that all we did with our focus on peak output was move revenue around. On one occasion, we sent an entire Australian sales team on an all-expenses-paid vacation in Las Vegas—such was the magnitude of their sales results! However, when they returned from their vacation, they went from the best- to the worst-performing team, and it took them months to spool back up again.

The net result in this—and other cases—was that we exchanged consistent sales for occasional sales bonanzas and, on average, reduced the profitability of the business. This, needless to say, is not entirely clever.

Your sales manager should manage sales just like a production environment. The goal should be to generate a steady volume of sales, month after month. Record months are only worth celebrating if it's likely that a new normal has just been achieved.

The Magic of the Twenty-Minute Stand-Up WIP Meeting

One of the first things I discovered when I emigrated to the United States was that pretty much every manufacturer runs a short stand-up WIP meeting at the start of every shift. (Similarly, most software environments run some variation of SCRUM meetings—which are similar in both design and function.)

We were quick to recognize the enormous value in these meetings and to replicate them in customer service and internal sales environments. WIP meetings are an extremely effective way of synchronizing the work within each of your teams—particularly work that is too granular to plan in a formal scheduling system; but, if you stagger them, WIP meetings are also an effective way of synchronizing the sales function and, indeed, the organization as a whole.

As well as being effective, WIP meetings are efficient. They consume very little time, and they provide management with insight that would otherwise be very difficult to gather.

A WIP meeting is a brief and carefully choreographed discussion of the work in progress. It should be conducted at exactly the same time every day, and each meeting should have exactly the same agenda.

Our normal approach is to stagger WIP meetings, working backward from production—and to have a participant in each meeting attend the next one in order to update the upstream team on notable outcomes. Most of our silent revolutionaries will have a team leader run each WIP with the responsible manager participating (and asking tough questions).

These meetings are always short (fifteen to thirty minutes), and the participants always stand for the duration of the meeting. (There's no such thing as a fifteen-minute sit-down meeting!)

Here's a typical agenda:

- a review of the status quo,
  - the total volume of open jobs (or sales opportunities),
  - the distribution of work among team members,
  - the status of queues (particularly, the pacesetter's buffer),
- a review of late-stage work,
  - opportunities that should be closing imminently (or should be abandoned),
  - customer service tickets that are in danger of running late, and
- agreement on action items (then disband the meeting).

General Sales Meetings

In addition to the daily WIP meetings, you must convene a weekly sales meeting that includes sales training (and role playing). If you have field sales-people, a daily stand-up WIP meeting tends to be impractical. Accordingly, my preference is for salespeople to attend this weekly sales meeting, along with their business-development coordinators and your campaign coordinator. Remote salespeople should attend via videoconference.

These sales meetings should be split into three components, with your campaign coordinator leaving after the first:

1. review the status quo (as in WIP meetings),
2. review late-stage opportunities, and
3. perform sales training.

Where the review of late-stage opportunities is concerned, your sales manager must ask tough questions to gain insight into exactly how the salespeople are conducting themselves on calls and to enable the team members to offer each other counsel. Sales training should consist primarily of role playing (as we discussed earlier).

MANAGEMENT INFORMATION

We discussed management information earlier, but an additional note is warranted. Because most of management's responsibilities are discharged in WIP meetings, it makes sense to design your management information system around your WIP meetings.

This means that your management information system should deliver answers to the following questions:

- How large are our queues of WIP?
- How many days' worth of appointments are scheduled in our field salespeople's calendars?
- How many days' worth of sales opportunities are queued upstream from each business-development coordinator and inside salesperson?
- How many days' worth of prospects are in the queue, awaiting promotional campaigns?
- How productive are our salespeople?
- What is the average throughput generated from each meaningful selling interaction?

- What is the velocity of our sales opportunities?
- For how many days are opportunities sitting at each stage in our sales workflow?
- What is the likelihood of late-stage opportunities converting into deals in the upcoming months?

In addition to this sales information, promotions needs answers to these questions:

- What return are we earning on our promotional spend (by campaign)?
- What does it cost (in promotional expenditure) to add a new contact to the house list?
- What does it cost (in promotional expenditure) to generate a sales opportunity?

FORECASTING (HOCUS POCUS WITH A DOLLAR SIGN)

I can't complete a chapter on management without touching on forecasting. *Forecasting* is an activity that consumes inordinate amounts of both sales managers' and salespeople's limited capacity, and in most cases, this time is completely wasted.

Actually, the reality is worse than that.

In most cases, the forecasting ritual generates misinformation that damages the relationships between sales and other functions. Forecasting, as it's typically practiced, reminds me of stories of the cargo cults on some Pacific Islands after World War II. The relatively primitive lifestyles of these islanders were interrupted by Japanese aircraft dropping large supplies of clothing, medicine, canned food, and tents to support the Japanese war effort. Some of these supplies were shared with the islanders, in exchange for their assistance.

After the war, when the planes and their valuable cargos disappeared, some of the islanders took to imitating the rituals they'd observed the Japanese performing. They carved headphones from wood and wore them while sitting in fabricated control towers, and they waved landing signals while standing on abandoned runways. Sadly, the re-creation of these rituals failed to stimulate additional airdrops of food and supplies!

The forecasting ritual imitates the objective (evidence-based) approach to management that sales leaders observe in other parts of the modern organization, but it fails to recognize the limitations of forecasting.

The Standard Approach to Forecasting

The standard approach to forecasting is very simple: Aggregate risk-adjusted estimates of future revenue from all salespeople and distribute the resulting number (the sum of all salespeople's estimates) to the rest of the organization to inform decision making.

So, if a given salesperson is working on three opportunities that they believe they will win next month, their calculus would look something like figure 42.

	Deal 1		Deal 2		Deal 3		
	$ 54,000.00		$ 26,500.00		$ 12,000.00		
	x 23%		x 75%		x 98%		
	$ 12,420.00	+	$ 19,875.00	+	$ 11,760.00	=	$ 44,055.00

Figure 42. How salespeople generate risk-adjusted estimates.

In case you're wondering where the weighting comes from, in many cases, salespeople simply supply a percentage that feels right. In other cases, this number is informed by the stage the opportunity is at in the opportunity management process. The latter approach only provides the perception of objectivity, however, because, it's generally the salesperson's opinion that determines when opportunities advance from one stage to the next. In some cases, sales managers will intercept these numbers and apply a discount to them to compensate for salespeople's natural optimism.

The problem here is fairly obvious. When you consider the incredible uncertainty baked into each of these numbers, you would need a massive sample size in order to create an estimating process that has any hope of yielding a meaningful number. And in most cases, because of the design of the traditional sales model, salespeople have only a handful of opportunities under management at any point in time.

A Better Approach

A better approach is to simply recognize that uncertainty and sample size conspire to make a statistical approach to forecasting impractical. Our silent revolutionaries have abandoned statistics (and the veneer of certainty) in favor of a more honest scenario-based approach.

Here's how that approach works: Management ensures that stages are aligned with objective customer behaviors, ignoring early stage opportunities altogether. In each sales meeting, late-stage opportunities are reviewed as a team and allocated to one of three categories: possible, probable, highly likely. The month in which each deal will likely close (if, indeed, it does) must be agreed on. This data is used to generate three month-by-month scenarios: the worst case (pessimistic, but not paranoid), the middle case, and the best case (optimistic, but not hysterical). This data must be made available (in summary form) to other departments—and you must refuse to collapse the data set into a single number.

In most cases, other managers will appreciate the sales department's newfound honesty. If the managers do push back, it's important to explain that collapsing these scenarios into a single number will destroy information, as opposed to creating it!

Considering that uncertainty is actually an attribute of the environment and not the sales manager, a set of scenarios will actually be more valuable to finance and other functions. This is because each decision that a manager makes has its own risk profile.

In some cases, managers must act primarily to avoid a downside (e.g., to avoid breaching customers' service-level agreements); and in other cases, their motivation is the pursuit of a gain of some kind. In each case, the managers will pay greater attention to one of the three scenarios.

Parting Words of Advice

With this book drawing to a close, it's over to you now! I'd like to leave you with some additional advice to guide you on your journey (notwithstanding the many pages of good advice dispensed thus far!).

Remember the Goal

Remember, the goal of a business is to make money—now and in the future. Making team members (including managers) happy is a necessary condition. Necessary conditions must always subordinate to the goal.

So, start with a clean sheet of paper and design your ultimate sales function without consideration of your existing team, and *then* determine how to transition to that sales function. If you attempt to do both simultaneously, you will end up designing what you already have, and your improvement initiative will be limited to adopting (and degrading) a new sales and marketing lexicon.

Customize Your Application of SPE, Not the Four Key Principles

If you must customize one of the applications of SPE described in this book, be sure that you do not violate any of the key principles. For example, if you partner your salespeople with business-development coordinators and then decide—for cultural reasons, perhaps—that you will retain performance pay for salespeople, you are in violation of one of the key principles.

Specifically, you are not centralizing scheduling if you are simultaneously paying one or more team members on a piece-rate basis. This one concession will be the undoing of your whole initiative. If it's not clear to both your salesperson and your business-development coordinator who owns the schedule, you will have conflict between them. This will result in your salesperson reclaiming their autonomy, and it will force your business-development coordinator to either shrink into the role of hapless assistant or (more likely) to resign.

Commit Absolutely

If you are going to make the kind of fundamental changes that are required to implement SPE, you should only proceed if you are prepared to commit (absolutely) to the future state.

If you are not fully committed, the skeptics among your team will sense it, and they will either resist passively or actively undermine the change initiative. If you are not fully committed, wait until you are. Alternatively, design a less ambitious future state (assuming it's possible to do that without contravening the point above!).

On the subject of commitment, if you're going to bet, bet big—not big enough to risk the company, but big enough to prove that you mean business and big enough to ensure that your change process doesn't take so long that it dies on the vine. For example, if you're building an inside sales team and your new team has just one person in it, you're not really building an inside sales team, are you? If you want proof of concept, you (or your executive assistant) can spend a day banging the phones and monitoring the reception you get. But once you have proof of concept, make a meaningful commitment.

Obsess over Activity Levels

People often ask me, "What should I measure?" no doubt expecting me to reel off a list of metrics. The truth is, early in your transition to the inside-out model, you should measure one thing only, and you should obsess over this number.

The metric (as I've already discussed) is sales activity or, more specifically, your volume of meaningful selling interactions. No matter what else happens, this number must go up, week after week, and it certainly must go up each time you make a change to your sales function.

Realistically, obsessing about your volume of meaningful selling interactions will force you to be mindful of other metrics too (e.g., the size of opportunity queues), but you don't have to worry about that right now.

Obsess over your volume of meaningful selling interactions, and everything else will look after itself.

Now, I know that the goal of a business is to make money—and that your meaningful selling interaction number doesn't have a dollar sign in front of it. But that's okay. This is a change initiative we're talking about here, not business as usual.

Because you're making radical changes—and because it takes a long time for the impact of those changes on sales numbers to manifest itself—it's critical that you have a faster feedback loop. You need a proxy for money. And meaningful selling interactions are it.

Inside Out, Not Outside In

Years ago, a director of sales at a silent revolutionary in Portland, Oregon, told me that SPE resonated with his management team because they've always believed in an *inside-out approach* to business. I appropriated that term on the spot—and I've been using it ever since.

Regardless of how many activities you perform in the field, SPE is fundamentally an inside-out approach to sales. Sales opportunities are originated inside. They are owned inside. All activities are planned inside. With SPE, the locus of sales is definitely inside.

Accordingly, when you plan and implement SPE, be sure to start inside and work outward, and not the other way around. More specifically, start at the factory door and work backward.

A second ago, I hung up the phone after counseling an executive who had just embarked on this journey. She was concerned that it wasn't possible to rapidly up-skill her customer service team with the capabilities required to manage inbound orders, generate quotes, and handle customer issues. I pointed out to her that this isn't the emergency that it seems to be. The fact is, someone in her organization is doing all that stuff right now. I encouraged her to identify the activity that occurs (or should occur) immediately prior to jobs entering production. (This activity is often what we call *prerequisite management*.) I advised her to first have her customer service team acquire *absolute mastery* over that activity. Once this has been achieved, the next activity in sequence can be transferred. And then the next.

By the time this executive has a truly robust customer service function, she'll have a much stronger base to build on, and she'll be much more confident taking her next steps.

This approach is the exact opposite of most sales improvement initiatives. Typically, sales improvement is more likely to start with a new comp plan or an expensive lead-generation campaign.

Ask for Help

It's true that SPE is a radical departure from standard practice, but that doesn't mean you're alone on your quest. There are silent revolutionaries on more than three continents who will be happy to provide advice.

If you have a question—or if you'd like to debate a contentious point— visit the forum at www.salesprocessengineering.net and create a new thread (comment) with your question.

Notes

1. Actually, in 2009, a Proudfoot study revealed that salespeople, internationally spend 11 percent of their time selling (with travel and administration claiming the lion's share). See: bit.ly/time-spent-selling.

2. The organization's customer-database and sales-management technology is typically referred to as *CRM*, and is a subset of enterprise resource planning (ERP) software.

3. Granted, *sales spectator* is not as sexy a role description as *sales manager*.

4. Technically, *sales* should be regarded as a subset of *distribution*, but because this book focuses on the former, I'm taking the liberty, on occasion, of using *sales* to refer to both.

5. Although, in some cases, interacting with a machine is preferable. I think most people would rather extract cash from an ATM—even if it means foregoing a relationship with a bank teller!

6. It is true that salespeople's relationships may assist in the sale of new product (or service) lines to existing accounts. However, it's more common than not to see salespeople neglecting *cross-selling* opportunities because they are so entangled in day-to-day customer service. The thing is that the two activity types (*customer service* and *sales*) tend not to comfortably coexist. In time, salespeople end up doing one or the other, rarely both.

7. Technically, the division of labor causes environments to become chaotic because of the complexity caused by a combination of resource dependency and variability in task completion time. To develop an understanding of the source of this chaos—as well as a method to tame it—read *The Goal* by Eliyahu Goldratt.

8. Intermediaries will tolerate channel conflict if the benefit they get from the principal's sales activity is greater than the cost (i.e., lost sales). This often occurs early in a product lifecycle, when the principal's high-profile sales activities accelerate the market growth (e.g., The Apple Store).

9. Google the phrase *regression to the mean.*

10. It's worth bearing in mind that labor is a particularly efficient market. Most employees know exactly what their fellow team members are earning as well as what they could earn at an alternative employer.

11. You can download a copy of my Visio workflow stencil from www .the-machine-book.com.

12. For more information on inbound marketing, see *Inbound Marketing: Get Found Using Google, Social Media and Blogs* by Brian Halligan and Dharmesh Shah (ISBN: 0470499311).

13. It is worth creating a custom footer containing a nice headshot for your business-development coordinators' emails.

14. Case in point: As I write, I'm tipping pretty much the entire contents of my brain into this book; I suspect, however, that on Amazon it will still sell for less than $20!

15. Actually, he didn't mention that prospects are prone to provide their phone numbers when requesting physical samples—but they are! *Scientific Advertising* should be compulsory reading for all business people; it's available for free online in numerous locations.

16. At the time of my writing, a Google search for "ERP productivity improvement" returns a link to 21,000 references from scholarly articles, followed by numerous vendor case studies citing measureable productivity improvement. A search for "CRM productivity improvement" returns numerous vendor articles promising productivity improvements but few (if any) citing quantitative outcomes. Amusingly, the second entry in those search results is a link to an article entitled "Why CRM sucks!" by yours truly!

17. By the way, my advice doesn't apply if you're a retailer and you need an Amazon-style website that is essentially a front-end for an ERP system. I'm assuming that not too many retailers will be reading this book.

18. If we encounter line managers, they tend to be customer service or inside sales team supervisors, and, more often than not, they are very capable.

19. Eli Goldratt defines *information* as the answer to the question asked. Absent the question, the data is just data!

20. You might want to start with *Developing Products in Half the Time*, by Smith and Reinertsen.

21. For your amusement, here's an example of a bridge that I internalized years ago, when I was selling insurance, and that I still can't prevent myself from using today: *In order to determine whether our service is going to make sense for your organization, I need to get your answers to three simple questions. Do you mind if I go ahead and ask them?*

About the Author

Justin Roff-Marsh is a sales management radical.

He takes issue with the starting assumptions that underpin the traditional approach to sales management and, consequently, rails against standard practices like salespeople's autonomous mode of operation, commission-based compensation, salespeople's ownership of accounts and much, much more!

In place of the traditional approach, he advocates that the sales function should be a 'machine', featuring the division of labor, the centralization of everything other than critical field visits and a formal approach to management.

After school, Justin rejected an offer from an engineering college and, instead, opted to study classical ballet full-time. While he loved ballet, he didn't care for the lifestyle of a dancer so he changed direction again.

He achieved immediate financial success as commissioned insurance salesperson then progressed rapidly to sales management. Before leaving the insurance industry he ran a team of 100 salespeople.

His next stop was a financial-services start-up and it was there that he developed his radical approach to sales. This approach contributed to the rapid growth of The Hudson Institute (Australia) which, in turn, prompted Justin to pine for his own business.

He founded Ballistix as a direct-marketing agency some 20 years ago and subsequently added consulting services. Today, Ballistix has clients in Australia, the United Kingdom and the United States of America. Justin emigrated to the USA in 2008 to lead Ballistix's growth there (and to hone his tennis game in the Californian sunshine!)

INDEX

management (*cont.d*)

management information, 149,
    222–223

management information systems
    (MIS), 192, 197

manufacturers' representatives, 92–93,
    95–96

manufacturing, history of, 109

marcoms, 207

marginal costing, 70

marketing
    automation, 192, 196
    communications, 163–165, 207
    departments, 43, 146
    functions, 163
    inbound, 160, 232
    management of, 206–207

Marketo, 196

markets, cold, 176

meetings, in workflow, 151

meetings, sales, 137, 220–222

metrics, 213, 227

Microsoft Access, 201

Microsoft CRM, 194

milestones, in workflows, 149

minor purchases, 40

MIS (management information
    systems), 192, 197

mobile-application-development firm,
    147

model, creating a
    business-development coordinators
        (BDC), 128
    business-development managers
        (BDM), 128
    campaign coordinators, 124–125
    customer service, 123–124
    economies of, 133–134
    example of, *f122*
    field specialists, 126–127
    identifying, 122–123
    inside sales, 124–125
    project leaders, 129–130
    regional offices, 131–133
    work in progress (WIP), 130–131

N

new product development (NPD), 77,
    78–80, 210

new service lines, 162

O

offers, promotional, 164–165, 167,
    174, 175, 176

office
    head, 37, 131–132
    regional, 131–133, 134

online advertising, 167, 178